SAVING JEMIMA

SAVING JEMIMA

Life and Love with a Hard-Luck Jay

Julie Zickefoose

Houghton Mifflin Harcourt
BOSTON   NEW YORK
2019

For information about permission to reproduce selections from this book, write
to trade.permissions@hmhco.com or to Permissions, Houghton Mifflin Harcourt
Publishing Company, 3 Park Avenue, 19th Floor, New York, New York 10016.

www.hmhco.com

Library of Congress Cataloging-in-Publication Data is available.
ISBN 978-1-328-51895-8

Excerpt on page 247 from *The Gift: Poems by Hafiz* by Daniel Ladinsky,
copyright 1999, and used with permission.

Book design by Martha Kennedy

Printed in China
TOP 10 9 8 7 6 5 4 3 2 1

For Bill, who gave me everything.

And for Phoebe and Liam, my two most successful releases.

CONTENTS

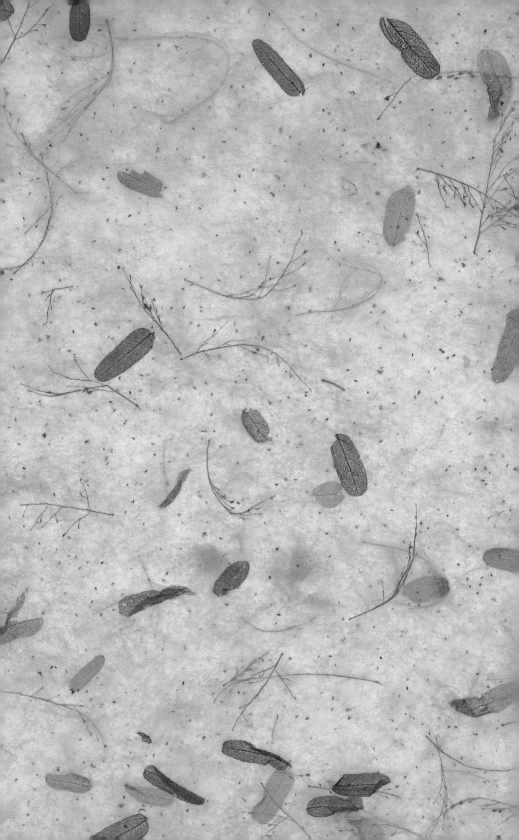

ACKNOWLEDGMENTS

Saving Jemima is different from anything I've produced before. My previous books have been compendiums of stories of the many birds and animals in my world. To follow the arc of one unique bird has been a big new adventure. My archetype in the effort was Joy Adamson's *Born Free,* a book I read and reread as a child, whose driving philosophy is returning a creature to the wild, whatever it takes.

To live inside this story and produce an illustrated docu-ment of Jemima's life, all within a year of when it happened, has been a sustained push like I've never before made. At times it's felt Sisyphean, but the fierce urgency was of my own making. As spring, summer, and autumn have rolled around, I wanted to paint Jemima in the seasonal settings that reflect exactly what's going on outside. The whole thrust in the writing, which I did as events unfolded, and the painting, which came later, has been to capture the spirit and immediacy of something fleeting, something that couldn't stay, any more than spring, summer, or autumn can stay. My aim was to give the reader a sense of what it's like to have one's life taken over by a bird, and then by the desire to see that bird again, and then by the need to figure out what just happened to me. I hope I conveyed why Jemima mattered so very much. She was far more than a blue jay to me. She was a beacon, guiding me into a place most people don't get to go: inside the mind of a wild bird. And becoming absorbed in her story got me out of my own head and doing my real work again, and for that I'll be forever grateful. So the first thank-you is to Jemima herself, for lighting my creative fuse, blasting me out of a trench, and opening the rollicking, ever-shifting, and mysterious world of blue jays to me.

Shawna and Sophia Linscott brought Jemima to me, likely never guessing all that would follow from that appeal for help. I thank them for caring for every living thing. Ornithologist Bob Mulvihill helped me understand what was going on with Jemima's molt cycle. I deeply appreciate his standing by with answers when I need them most. David Schroder offered his extensive files on blue jay migration and shared insights on blue jay vocalizations.

Lesley the Bird Nerd is anything but; she's a field researcher of the first order, doing groundbreaking observational work, which she gives away for the joy of sharing. The Theissen family's joy in maintaining a relationship with free-flying Gracie is infectious and also generously shared. Carrie Barron gave me a peek into the jay mind with the amazing Conrad, as did Pamela and Natalie Sezov and their beloved Tweeters. And Harvey Webster of the Cleveland Museum of Natural History gave me a hands-on experience with imprinting in blue jays that I could never have grasped in theory. We all have been touched, lifted, and lit up by these higher beings in our lives.

My dear friend Robert F. Giddings, DVM, is my first resort in bird medicine. Erica Miller, DVM, and Sallie Welte, VMD, have been generous with their time and advice, and certainly saved Jemima's life. Jessica Kidd, DVM, swooped in to help me on the home front. Fellow wildlife rehabilitator Melanie Furr has been a constant presence of empathy and hope. And the Ohio Wildlife Center, particularly Kristi Krumlauf and Stormy Gibson, have my enduring gratitude for always doing their best by wildlife and people too. OWC gives Ohioans a place to turn when we can't walk by a suffering creature, and that is a service beyond valuing. I thank them for entrusting me with Josie, Caledonia, and Lou in the summer of 2018. Their bratty jay spirit infused my paintings and healed something that had been left open in me.

I thank Mark Carroll and Ann Prum of Coneflower Studios for filming Jemima into posterity for PBS *Nature*. The experience taught me that the more you want a blue jay to do something, the less likely it is to do it.

On the writing front, many people helped me get it all down. Invaluable guidance on the direction of the manuscript (and life in general) came from Caroline Quine. My "Charlotte," Kristin Macomber helped pull me out of a large tangle of science and words, reminding the Science Chimp that more detail is not always better. Love and support from Anne Babcock, Kyle and Geoff Heeter, Mimi Hart, Tim Ryan, Donna Quinn, Ann Hoffert, Cindy House, Jayne Trapnell, Tanya Wilder, David Fleming, Mary Jane Helgren, and James Adams lights my life. Stalwart daily wisdom and healing love from Shila Wilson keeps me right side up in choppy water.

I thank my agent, Russell Galen, for instantly grasping what was special about Jemima's story, and my editor, Lisa White, for her patient support, ever-ready presence, and warm enthusiasm for this project. She kicked the door back open, let me add Chapter 20 after deadline, and let me rewrite the Epilogue three times. I'll always be grateful. Martha Kennedy, who designed the book, is a joy to work with. The honor of having HMH's Adult Trade Art Director put a blue jay book together is not lost on me. Copy editor Ana Deboo caught errors and repetitions like an all-star shortstop. There is nothing quite like turning one's work over to a publisher like Houghton Mifflin Harcourt, knowing it will be handled with exacting care. I thank Gary Sinclair for speaking my color language, and bending over backward to please a fussy artist with the scans he executed.

My Zickefoose siblings, Barbara, Bob, Nancy, and Micky, give me stability and support: a family foundation that's strong, solid, and loving. Bill Thompson III stepped in to feed Jemima, take some crucial photos, and comfort me when things got hairy. It was he, after all, who brought me to this beautiful place, worked to build it up from nothing, and gave me the two best kids anyone could ask for. Bill, I will always be grateful for the chance to make a homestead and bring up children with you in Appalachian Ohio. Liam and Phoebe had the patience and presence to be Jemima's flock while she needed one. They kept me here in the world of humans when my woodland friends were trying to spirit me away. And it's they who led me to the hole in the garden wall, and pulled me through.

May 16, 2016
The Egg that started it all: blue jay egg from a clutch of 5, 2 of which were taken by a chipmunk.

Looking at this egg, I feel I'm holding a blue jay in my hand.

ONE

The Egg

IT ALL STARTED with an egg, as many things do: birds, turtles, platypuses. This time, what began was a notion, born of curiosity. It was the kind of curiosity that flames up when one stops to contemplate something so perfect and mysterious as a bird's egg. It's something we can't open, something we aren't given to understand, this capsule of liquid protein, encased in a glossy shell, that will, given time and warmth, produce a squirming bird. For some reason I can't remember, I was on my hands and knees under a spreading Japanese maple in my southeast Ohio yard. It was May 16, 2016. And there in the grass beneath the maple was an egg, fresh and beautiful, an aqueous olive drab ground color, speckled and splotched with lilac, brown, and black.

Our house on Indigo Hill, an 80-acre wildlife sanctuary in southeast Ohio, May 22. Jemima's Japanese maple throws shade in the side yard.

"Now, that's a blue jay egg," I said, not really knowing how I knew it. I just knew it. My brain did an instant sorting of variables, such as size, color, shape, and what species might lay an egg like this in a rural Ohio yard, and spat out "blue jay." I looked straight up, knowing the egg had to come from a nest. And I saw the white-spangled tail of a blue jay sticking out over the edge of a lopsided mess of twigs and vines and straw in the top canopy of the maple. I couldn't believe that there was a jay nesting so close to the house, that I hadn't known she was there, and most of all that she was sitting stolidly on her nest with me on hands and knees only eight feet below.

I cupped the egg in one hand and trundled quietly on three limbs toward the house, rising up only when I was out of the bird's startle zone. With a flashlight held up behind it in a dark hallway, I held it in the curl of my fingers, shining the light through it, candling it. There was a yellow yolk floating in clear albumen. It was freshly laid, with no embryo visible as yet. I figured it rolled out of the nest, which looked a bit tilted, or even blew out when the jay wasn't sitting. I decided to put it back.

This involved waiting for the incubating bird to leave; a step-ladder, Bill holding it tightly; and me climbing higher than I wanted to. Before I replaced the egg, I decided to take a photo of the nest. Lo and behold, there were two other eggs lying on the shallowest platform of black rootlets I'd ever seen. It wasn't even a salad plate; it was a saucer. How did those eggs stay in the nest long enough for her to sit on them? Humbled as I generally am by the engineering and artistry of bird nests, I knew this was a crummy nest. I put the egg back anyway and hoped for the best.

Because I'm rarely content to hope for the best, I was soon launching a plan to protect the nest from climbing predators. I needed to get some sort of predator baffle around the tree's trunk. I didn't stop to wonder how the jay might fare without this intervention; I just forged ahead with my plan. That perfect egg, the vision of the bird growing within it, had set me on a crusade.

Early the next morning, the jay's tail was still protruding over the nest rim, so I took off for a Home Depot thirty miles away, coming home with four long rectangular "lawn chutes" made of lightweight corrugated plastic. My idea was to construct a slick barrier to any climbing predator. I was kneeling beneath the maple, wrestling the chutes into place around the tree's curvy trunk, when I saw some tiny eggshell fragments in a little pile in the grass, right where I'd found the egg yesterday. They were sticky with albumen. The little pile of shards told me that the deed was most likely done by a chipmunk who had climbed the tree, stuffed the egg in a cheek pouch, then climbed down to feast in the grass. Rats, rats, rats. Or: chipmunks, chipmunks, chipmunks. They are not the adorable sprites their appearance would have you believe. They're bloodthirsty and hell on birds and their nests.

The incubating jay was nowhere to be seen. I pulled out

the stepladder and climbed up to see if I could find any more clues. There, teetering on the edge of the nest, was a lone egg, stone cold. I knew the chipmunk would come back for it, and I couldn't bear the thought. I picked it up and climbed back down the ladder.

I walked around the front yard with the egg, photographing it, admiring its color and sheen. Every pigment here — the green, brown, black, and lilac — was derived from blood and bile, painted in tiny spurts from the female jay's uterine wall, the scrawls formed when the egg turned as it was being painted. I was seized with the desire to paint my living room this precise shade of khaki gold green, then spatter the walls with mummy brown, sepia, lavender. The perfection of it had grabbed my imagination. In this small oval object, an inch and an eighth long, was encoded everything blue jay. In my hand I held a blue jay. I suddenly wanted so badly to hatch a blue jay, to give the embryo inside this egg a chance to become what it was meant to be.

I had felt this urge before but had the sense never to follow it. I've had people write and ask me how to hatch an egg they've found on their lawn, and I always answer that even if

It's hard to believe the shimmering colors of a blue jay egg are derived from blood and bile.

it were legal for the average person to do such a thing, they are almost guaranteed to fail at it somewhere along the line. Best to just leave it there. Who hatches an egg and raises a bird that was never meant to be? I wasn't stupid; I was besotted, taken by a notion. Isn't this how art and inspiration work? Art is a tease, a temptress, a joker with a keen sense of irony and no regard for timing.

How could I let the egg go cold and die? I set it on my drawing table, cradled in tissues, and sent an email to my friend Dave McShaffrey, a professor at Marietta College and purveyor of all gear biological. Might he have an incubator? I knew, even as I sent the message, that I was crazy to think I could hatch this fresh blue jay egg, much less raise the baby from Day 1. There were doubtless dietary requirements I wouldn't be able to duplicate, even if it hatched. But I had to try. I wanted badly to draw the chick from life as it developed, to continue the work with nestling birds featured in my last book, *Baby Birds: An Artist Looks into the Nest*. Blue jays are the most skittish and wary of birds. There was no way I'd ever be able to peek into a blue jay nest again, no way to baffle one if I found one I could reach. And I couldn't work with an unprotected nest, vulnerable to climbing predators. If I was ever going to draw the development of a baby blue jay, I knew I'd have to raise it myself. The probability that the chick would imprint on me flitted through my mind. *I'll worry about imprinting and release later, I guess. Jays are so smart, it should be able to make its way and find its own kind, right?* I was putting the cart before a considerable horse, and I knew it. But this vision of studying and painting a baby jay only pulled me forward.

On Wednesday, May 18, I drove into town to pick up the incubator, which was equipped with an automatic egg-turner (a blessing for an egg that incubates for as long as sixteen to eighteen days). I got it going Wednesday evening, filled the hu-

midity runnels, and saw that it was holding a steady temperature, and on the morning of Thursday, May 19, I refilled the
humidity wells with filtered water and ceremoniously installed
the egg. Standing at room temperature for a day or so wouldn't
harm it, especially in such an early stage of incubation. It all
seemed so very magical and the possibility that it would work
so very distant that there was an air of surreality about the proceedings. I just couldn't believe that this little capsule might
hold the makings of a blue jay that I could raise.

On May 20 (let's call this Day 3, since the mother jay incubated it for at least a day), I decided to candle the egg again
to see if there were any changes. Instead of a yellow yolk, I saw
a cloudy area that could very well have been a developing embryo. Or perhaps blood vessels around the yolk. I didn't know.
I just knew it was changing. And I knew that an infertile egg
would show a bright yellow yolk, like it did when it was very
fresh.

On the evening of May 23, my son, Liam, and I candled
first an infertile Carolina wren egg (we could see the yellow
yolk and clear albumen) and then the blue jay egg. It had been
incubating for six days. I asked him what he could see in each
egg. Carolina wren: "The yolk, and clear." In the blue jay egg:
"Nothing." It was dark, opaque. We couldn't see the light shining through it. The portent of this change shot down to the
soles of my feet. There was someone in there now.

I checked the temperature neurotically, and it was good
to be a bit neurotic about it, because sometimes it would read
102 degrees, and sometimes it read 98, and it all seemed to depend where the tip of the temperature sensor was located. This
made me nervous, using a still-air incubator, having to wonder
whether I was cooking the precious orb. Still, something good
seemed to be happening. It was developing. Perhaps I was going to be a blue jay mama.

On May 25 at 10:15 p.m., I decided to make a real candling rig. I cut a pea-sized hole out of a piece of mat board and made a ring of white tape to hold the egg in place. This would concentrate light in a small spot on the egg. I was moving the egg around over the light and couldn't see much until I realized I was seeing an area perhaps the size of a navy bean and it was MOVING and jumping around! I freaked out, all the way out, and called everyone into the little room to see. I just couldn't believe it. There was a living soul in that egg. I knew it, but I didn't *know* it until I saw it moving. It was like the rush I got when I saw my first child Phoebe's fetal heart beating on an ultrasound screen. It was awe, it was rapture; it was fear and joy, mingled.

On the morning of May 26, I woke up thinking about Liam, who was displaying some curious, or perhaps typical, behavior for a sixteen-year-old boy. He was retreating from a beautiful girl from another school who was crazy about him, because he said he didn't want to impinge on his creative time. He wanted to draw whenever he wanted to; he worried that she'd expect a lot from him if he took the leap. I wondered if he'd be afraid to go to college. I wondered if he'd want to live at home forever. Had I messed up here? Just the usual early morning mother-angst, with a weird ornithological segue. My thoughts turned to the blue jay egg. What if, against all odds, it hatched, and imprinted on me, and couldn't function as a jay? What if it turned out to be unreleasable, and had to be kept confined for the rest of its life? I couldn't imagine that, geared as I am to release the birds that I raise — more than twenty species to date. I wondered if, raised in isolation from its kind, it would know it was a jay; if, when the migratory urge struck, it would instinctively flock with others who shared its voice, its brilliant colors. I imagined how invested I'd be by then, having raised it from Day 2 of incubation. I wondered if I would be able to keep it warm, to feed it the right things, to keep it healthy. I'd never done this, hatched an egg. I wondered what I didn't know. It seemed, there in the dark, that what I didn't know was . . . everything.

I opened the incubator that evening, the ninth day of incubation, to check the temperature, and I smelled something different. To my horror, I found that the humidity wells had gone dry, for how long I didn't know. I had overfilled them four days earlier, and the incubator had leaked, so I hadn't added water since. I dribbled a few drops of water on the egg. I fretted and paced. And finally decided to candle the egg. It had changed a lot. I could now see a large yolk with a dark ring around it. I emailed biology professor Katy Lustofin of Marietta College, who opined that the dark ring could indicate bacterial growth. She reassured me that letting the incubator go without water would not necessarily kill the egg. However, the bacteria could have been in the egg from the start, only just getting going now to do their dirty work. Bacteria getting into an egg . . . though I'd never thought about the possibility, it would become a recurring theme over the next year. Katy told me to wait and see if there was any change, or any movement over the next few days.

Over the next two days, there was no change, no movement; the embryo had died. The albumen remained clear, the ring was stalwart; there was no movement from the little jumping bean inside. My journal entries end bleakly:

"Here the log ends. I don't even have the energy to write about how I felt when that egg died."

Even with the remove of a year, the sadness is still palpable. I know it was only a blue jay egg that would otherwise have gone into a chipmunk's stomach; in the grand scheme, it was only usable protein. But I can't help but build castles in the air. It's what humans do. I laid aside my dream of watching an egg tooth make the first break through its shell, of sitting poised to give the first feeding to an intelligent being who would believe from that moment on that I was its mother. I would not be sketching it or trying to capture its exact skin shade of grayish pink in watercolors. I don't care if that seems like a weird dream. It was mine, and it had died aborning.

May 16, 2017

On the mulch outside
St. Mary's School, a young jay
waits for parents who will not
be back. Marion St, Marietta, OH

TWO

Facebook Waif

THE NEXT YEAR went by like a hurtling train, with me selling, signing, boxing, and sending nearly a thousand copies of *Baby Birds* out of my studio, and promoting it in twenty-three speaking engagements around the country. Natural history authors like me aren't sent on all-expense-paid book tours. In the publishing industry, we're considered niche writers with a comparatively narrow audience. I negotiate book speaking engagements and drive myself there, having bought the books I sign and sell after each talk. I wind up loading many thirty-six-pound boxes of them in and out of my car, with no roadies in sight. I'm usually my own tech support, setting up and troubleshooting the

An eleven-day-old blue jay waits for parents who will not be coming back. St. Mary's School, Marion Street, Marietta, Ohio, May 16, 2017.

projector and PA system for my shows at fellowship halls, ho-
tels, and conference centers. I've spoken in university lecture
rooms and hotel ballrooms, galvanized sheds and festival tents
decked with straw-bale seating. I produce and mat my own art
prints, sell note cards and even a jigsaw puzzle with my art on
it, along with the four books I've written to date. It's a load, a
roadshow. It's my life.

The spring of 2017 was jammed with travel, from Florida
to Virginia to California, back to West Virginia, with Ohio engagements sprinkled throughout. I was moving a lot of books,
sustaining a yearlong effort, but I was tired — soul-tired. I kept
reminding myself that giving talks and selling books was as vital
a part of my work as writing and painting, but there was a growing ache in my creative heart. I missed being home. I needed
to get back to my true work. I was worried about my daughter,
Phoebe, who was overextended in a grueling spring semester
as an earth and oceanographic science major at Bowdoin College. I could hear in her voice that she was hanging by her nails,
navigating the choppy waters of her first relationship breakup
even as she powered through final exams. I was fighting battles

Solitude encourages reflection and productivity, if you're prepared for it.
(Michele Coleman Photography)

of my own, buffeted by losses that came in waves as regular as the sea's. Phoebe's breakup hit me like a train; it felt for all the world as if I'd adopted a beloved son, then had to give him back. My reliable furry support system needed support of his own: I was dancing the senior dog waltz with my beloved Chet Baker, a Boston terrier who, at twelve, was running out of heart and spirit. I was surviving but feeling lonely and unsupported.

While I was preparing to become a mother jay in 2016, I applied for and received a scientific collecting permit from the State of Ohio and the US Fish and Wildlife Service. This would replace the wildlife rehabilitation and salvage permit I'd held since 1992. Both allowed me to work with songbirds and their nestlings. The key difference between them was that the scientific permit allowed me a little privacy. A requirement for holding a wildlife rehab permit was having your home telephone number publicly listed. The resulting calls from all over Ohio, about everything from orphaned fawns to box turtles, bats, and baby birds, had reduced me to cringing every time the phone rang. As a lone rehabilitator without veterinary backup or elaborate housing, I was in no position to take in even a tiny percentage of the orphaned and injured wildlife concerned. But I spent a lot of time advising, referring, and facilitating the care and transfer of these broken, lost creatures. In fall and winter, when baby bird calls finally ceased, busted-up hawks and owls took their place. These I found the most challenging and dispiriting, because nothing good happens when a speeding car meets a flying raptor. All I could do was tell people how to handle and feed them, take some in for temporary care, and try to arrange transport for all of them to the Ohio Wildlife Center, the state's largest wildlife rehabilitation organization, two and a half hours away.

So it was a relief to have the phone fall blessedly silent

when my rehabilitation permit expired and my name was taken off the public rehabilitator lists. But it was a short-lived peace.

Social media abhors a vacuum. I can't escape the barrage of Facebook messages pleading for help with baby birds. People merrily tag me in their friends' posts as the baby bird factotum, without a thought to the ripple effect set in motion. They're delighted, with a few keystrokes, to present a real live expert to a friend who's just found a baby bird. They're done. It's then left to me to respond in detail to dozens of queries that all start with "I found a baby bird. What do I do?" The resulting exchanges can go on for hours and often days. Multiply that by the number of inquiries that roll in, and it doesn't take long to get overwhelmed.

The pickle I'm in is real. I depend on social media to promote my work, my speaking engagements, my books. My blog, Facebook, and Instagram have become the powerful advertising right arm of my business, one whose message I can control and direct. I need to maintain an online presence to promote and sell my books. But along with that convenience and outreach comes access. The real hazard of Facebook and, to a lesser extent, Instagram is two-pronged. First is the instantaneous ease with which thousands of people can access each other (and me). Second, and far deadlier, is the visual element. It's one thing to get a phone call about a lost baby bird. It's quite another to get a photo of it. That's okay when the bird is in Seattle. There's no way it's going to become my problem to care for. When the bird is nearby and I know there's no one else within a two-hour drive who will help, I'm sunk. It's a dart to the heart, one I'm helpless to deflect or resist.

It was exactly one year to the day from when I'd been crawling around under the Japanese maple and found the jay egg lying in the grass — May 16, 2017 — that I got a Facebook message that would change everything. Shawna Linscott, from

Marietta, Ohio, had found a baby blue jay in the middle of the street.

> *Hello Julie, this is Shawna Linscott from Marietta. In the past you've helped me with a turtle and a bird. This little fella has been on the ground outside of my daughter's school since 9:30 this morning. It appears it has not moved from under the bush where I placed it. As I approached it to get this photo it was opening its mouth for food, so I have no idea if the mother has returned to feed. My question to you is, do I leave it, or do I take it home?*

I was sunk the moment I saw this photo of a nestling blue jay in need. May 16. (Shawna Linscott)

A photo of a jay, perhaps eleven days old, its eyes dull and sunken with dehydration, drew a gasp from me. Quickly I typed:

> *Look up in the tree and trees nearby for a twiggy nest. Are there jays yelling at you? If they are yelling at you, they are aware of it. It doesn't look good, though. It's too young to be out of the nest. Ideally you return it to the nest. I know that isn't always possible. It hasn't moved because it's really too young to go anywhere. Cat food or soaked kitten chow is*

a good food. Needs nourishment and liquids. Ultimately if it can't be returned to the nest it should go to Columbus. I'm driving up on the 20th and could take it.

Shawna responded:

> *No jays that I have seen, only robins. Did not see a nest.*
> *As far as liquids do I just give water? And how often do I need to give liquids and food? I will get a cat carrier and return and get it. I will do everything I can to help this little fella and yes if you could take it to Columbus on the 20th that would be great!*

I scrutinized the photo. The bird was in trouble, as any baby bird who had gone without food all day would be. It didn't look good. I couldn't tell Shawna how to save this little life. There are some things you have to do yourself. I got up, paced around in a circle, took a deep breath, and typed,

> *You might want to bring it to me, Shawna. Jays are difficult. Need to be fed at least once an hour. Water's OK in small amounts. Better to just bring it to me.*

At that point I was thinking I'd feed it for a few days, then relinquish it to the Ohio Wildlife Center when I drove up to Columbus to pick up Phoebe for a three-week summer break at home. I no longer was the woman who, a year ago, fell under the spell of a mystical green egg and thought she wanted to hatch and raise a blue jay. I had things to do, places to go, changes coming in my life that were taking my full attention. I wasn't up for a several-month commitment to a needy bundle of fluff. I instructed Shawna to feed it as much scrambled egg as it would eat before loading it in the carrier and taking it to the *Bird Watcher's Digest* office so Bill could bring it home to me.

I mixed some powdered nestling formula with water and went to the basement to get the two plastic shoeboxes that held my live mealworm culture. Yes, I keep live mealworms going in the basement for just such emergencies. Two days earlier, a bizarre urge had come over me to clean the mealworms, a disgusting job that involves sieving them in a stiff breeze and often getting covered with frass. After thirty-five years of raising and handling mealworms, I've developed an allergy to them, so I dislike this necessary ritual. I smiled as I picked up the immaculate bins of clean, well-fed mealworms, and wondered at the coincidence.

Our eyes met, and I discarded my plan to turn the baby over to the Ohio Wildlife Center. I'd raise this one myself. May 16.

When Bill arrived, I opened the carrier and picked up the young jay. It was virtually tailless, a compact, stub-winged gray bundle, trimmed in military blue and white. It fit neatly in my palm, and it was absolutely charming, as these cobby little avian prototypes tend to be. But I sensed I had my work cut out for

me with this bird; it was dehydrated and "down," in the parlance of avian rehabilitators, and in fact it kept its eyes closed
for most of the first three days I had it. It would gape for food
with vigor only first thing in the morning. I had to force-feed
it the rest of the time. I knew jays to be vigorous beggars and
enthusiastic eaters and sensed that there was something off.
On the third day, its droppings turned an alarming shade of sea
green. Not sure what that was about, but feeling it was nothing good, I started it on Baytril, hoping that whatever was bugging it might be knocked out by this wide-spectrum antibiotic.
I refrained from naming it, telling myself that I was waiting
for Phoebe to pronounce on its sex and choose a name. She'd
proven a fey prognosticator of the sex of many baby birds. But
mostly I was afraid this little bird wouldn't make it.

  With Baytril, the bird brightened and kept its eyes open
more. Its droppings normalized, and it showed a little more interest in food. Each morning, it was a bit livelier when it greeted
me, and the sound of keening hunger calls gladdened my heart.
It began to clamber around and preen, always a good sign of
well-being in birds. I retrofitted a painted wicker Easter basket
with strips of soft toweling along the edge and paper towels in
the center. It made a fine nest, dropping catcher, and carrier for
the little jay, who soon learned to flutter-climb atop the handle

Soft, padded perches prevent bumblefoot and encourage napping.

for a better look at its world, which at this point was my kitchen. Being fairly heavy birds, blue jays given only hard perching surfaces are prone to pressure sores on their feet. These can provide an entry point for a staph bacterium that causes a fatal disease called bumblefoot. Needless to say, I quickly padded its favorite perches in plush cloth.

May 20, the day I'd planned to take it to the Ohio Wildlife Center, came and went. I'd fallen for its winsome personality, for the challenge of bringing it back to health and releasability. I wanted to be the one to see it through release. And with that decision, my transformation back into the egg-contemplating madwoman was complete. Bill and Liam made the two-hour drive to nab Phoebe at the airport. I had a new mission: to stay home and take care of this baby jay.

I knew from our phone conversations that Phoebe was riding a ragged emotional edge and had been for weeks. She'd worked too hard, proving to herself and the world that multivariate calculus would not be her academic Waterloo. She'd been staying up far too late and worrying too much. She'd navigated a heartbreakingly difficult and complicated breakup without having the time or mental space to process what had taken place. I was braced to receive her. I'd cleaned the house, washed her bedding and hung it out in the fresh air, laid in all her favorite foods and planned meals intended to make her swoon with delight: Chicken pot pie. Roast beef with gravy and green beans. Carnitas. Three-cheese ravioli sautéed in sage. Homegrown salads. For the next three weeks, I was planning to feed her, listen to her, and let her sleep until noon if that was what she wanted. She was all grown up, but she was still mine to care for, and I meant to care for her. She'd get Mama's medicine in every home-cooked meal, in every undisturbed hour of peaceful sleep.

Even with advance warning, I still wasn't ready for the

hollow-eyed ghost of my daughter who stumbled in the door, tears already carrying mascara into her freckles. I held her as she wept with joy and relief, and when her slender rib cage was no longer heaving, I turned to open the jay's carrier. Though it was late at night, I took the small gray baby on my finger and gently transferred it to hers. She raised it to her face and buried her nose in its soft feathers, breathing in its woodsy scent. She bent her head and laid her cheek against the bird's back, smiling through her tears. "You always have a friend for me when I come home." I shrugged, wiped my own tears, and wrapped my arms around them both.

First encounter: Phoebe meets the orphaned jay. May 20.

I had yet to name the bird, and I had a guess at its sex, but I wanted to see what Phoebe thought. The next day, we all convened at the kitchen table to name the jay. The scent of blueberry pancakes and maple syrup still hung in the air. I'd cut a big bouquet of irises, white with lilac ruffles, which dominated the table with their beauty and grapey fragrance. "Iris," Phoebe said. "I think it's a female, and I want to name her Iris." There were murmurs around the table. "I like Iris, and I concur on its sex. I think it's a female, too. But I was kind of thinking about a name that started with 'J,'" I said. We ran through some names beginning with "J," until Bill, who had, after all, named our Boston terrier after jazz artist Chet Baker, said, "I think we should call her Jemima."

Jemima Iris Jay. The name had sprung right off the breakfast table. It was a relief to have something to call the wee thing, to frame our affection for her with a name and a guess at her sex. In fact, there is no reliable visual way to tell male blue jays from female; they appear identical to human eyes. Surely jays have ways to instantly tell each other's sex. There must be behavioral, vocal, and plumage clues, hidden to us, that blue jays can perceive. Are the ultraviolet shades in their blue plumage different to their sensitive eyes? Maybe there's a code in the soft conversational calls that pass between them when they're together. Or perhaps there's a method by which they determine each other's sex that's undreamt of by mere humans. There was so much I wondered about blue jays. The more I work with birds, the more I believe in the undreamt, the things we are not given to know.

sweet corn, raw

The Things She Ate

mealworm-
freshly
molted only 1

Mulberries

pine nuts

painted lady

walnuts

Jemima, Day 25

mealworms

Chicken & rice

Strawberries

raspberries

blueberries

Japanese
beetle

mealworm
pupae

pecans

Snap peas

THREE

Fledging and Feeding

BLUE JAYS FLEDGE, or leave the nest, around Day 17. A baby jay is much more portable and easier to handle before this developmental landmark; it'll sit around like a chair in the hall, parked wherever you put it. Droppings emerge in neat fecal sacs and can be caught with strategically placed paper towels. After the nestling makes the leap and becomes a fledgling, it'll be fluttering, hopping across the floor, cheeping, and leaving spots of whitewash wherever it goes. It's a toddler, up and running without a diaper. This is the point at which I put up the fledging tent. Intended as a temporary shelter, usually around a picnic table, nylon screen tents with built-in floors are a god-

The things she ate. Jemima tasted a great variety of foods, but these were her favorites.

send for the avian rehabilitator. They are the cheapest, easiest way to contain a songbird, to give it ample room to exercise without damaging its feathers or breaking a bone.

Like so many imported products, screen tents get flimsier every year. I miss my sturdy old fifteen-foot-by-seventeen-foot beast, which was destroyed by a sudden summer derecho. I saw it crumpled up and rolling across the lawn, aluminum poles and all. The model currently in use, called the Zephyr, is well named, because the slightest breeze threatens to carry it away. The door zippers are of a gauge one might select not for a tent but for a cocktail dress, so they've given out, and the doors are held with clothespins now. Because it can't take wind, I set it up in our detached garage, with one end exposed to the air and sun. My birds can exercise, play, sunbathe, and get a good feel for the sounds and sights of the world before they're released.

Phoebe and I spent a morning setting the tent up, with padded perches, water, and food dishes for the time when Jemima would be self-feeding. Installed in the tent, seventeen-day-old Jemima seemed only to wilt, and she spent the hours alone sleeping, preening, or simply staring quietly out into the woods. Welcomed back into the house, she perked up, begged for food, hopped across the carpet, pooped, and clambered around on lamps and furniture. Mostly, though, she sought company, which Phoebe, twenty-one, and her brother Liam, seventeen, were happy to provide. I was working in the studio when their voices rang out. "Mom! Come see what Jemima can do!" Working with the little jay's desire to perch high, the kids had devised a game in which they encouraged Jemima to hop from the floor to a leg, to a raised arm, to another arm held a couple of feet higher, until she'd navigated in stages all the way up to eye level. They called it "Jungle Jem." If a bird could be proud of itself, that stub-tailed jay was. She grasped the concept immediately and seemed to enjoy the challenge of flutter-

Chet Baker interrupts a game of Jungle Jem with an unequivocal bid for attention.

hopping higher and higher, along with the praise and applause that accompanied her feat. Jays love a parade.

Fledging, it should be clear by now, means only leaving the nest, which is not the same thing as attaining independence. From a bird rehabilitator's point of view, fledging is comparable to the moment a baby stands up, totters across the floor, and becomes a toddler. That baby's not feeding herself or calling home on Sundays. She's still entirely your problem. It means that things just got a little messier and more hazardous. Though she'd fledged, it would be weeks before Jemima was ready for release.

It was clear that Jemima craved a flock. If she was sitting quietly in the kitchen, and we all got up and walked around the corner into the living room, the little jay would give a quavering *Kreeee?* and take wing, following us as if her life depended on it. It was endearing, and it contrasted with most other birds I've raised, who, as long as they were well-fed, seemed unconcerned about my whereabouts until their tanks were empty again. It was here that the specter of imprinting materialized, with dark predictions from one Facebook friend who'd raised several corvids that Jemima could imprint on people and turn out to be a less-than-functional wild bird as a result. Imprinted birds may spurn their own kind and select humans as their partners once they reach sexual maturity. This can be inconvenient if the imprinted bird is a crow, or dangerous if it's a great horned owl that tries to copulate with your head. Members of the family Corvidae (jays, crows, magpies, and ravens) are highly intelligent, social birds, vulnerable to imprinting. Needless to say, I was hoping to avoid imprinting as the outcome of raising Jemima. "You're going to have to change your strategy from the bluebirds you're used to raising," my acquaintance warned. I cocked an eyebrow. No one who raises birds should treat each species the same; the bird leads you with its demands and demonstrated needs, until you arrive at a strategy that works. Never having raised a corvid, I was feeling my way, but I was feeling my way with sensitive hands.

Jemima's relationship with Liam, seventeen, was quietly companionable.

Having done rehab in some form since I was a kid in Virginia, I've raised nestlings of seventeen songbird species and kept another twenty-five species, both passerines and non-passerines, as adults. It's a varied list, with a representative or two from most songbird families, and a few float up as having been particularly challenging to raise. Chimney swifts and ruby-throated hummingbirds needed special feeding, housing, and prolonged care; eastern phoebes were particularly delicate; brown thrashers were catlike and comical. Rose-breasted grosbeaks, northern cardinals, mourning doves, wood thrushes, and gray catbirds stand out for being pleasant and affectionate. The summer before I met Jemima, a tiny Carolina wren fledgling, a pecan-sized bird packed with brains and personality, stole our hearts clean away. Each bird had its own arc, each its own story, and all have informed my approach to the next young thing that comes into my care. The answer to the question of whether Jemima would imprint on me would have to wait until her release.

I was surprised when, only eighteen days old, Jemima cocked her head, reached out, and plucked two mealworms off the tweezers, masticating and swallowing them as if it were no big deal. That seemed quite precocious, given that eastern bluebirds gape vigorously, and don't even think about plucking food out of the tweezers until around Day 25. But there was a lot about this bird that was different from others I'd raised. I'd never seen a bird taste food like Jemima did. She'd run her triangular pink tongue out and *lick* any new food offered her. Her tongue would flicker in and out, and she'd get a thoughtful, faraway look in her eyes as she considered its flavor. If it passed the taste test, Jem would take a tiny portion, running it around in her bill with her tongue, and usually flinging it aside without swallowing it. She acted as if she thought I might be trying to poison her, but as I watched her, I wondered what sophisticated chemical analysis might be going on between her obviously sensitive taste buds and her brain.

Omnivores, it turns out, are really fun to feed. The first plate I offered Jemima, once she started picking up her own food, included banana cake, fresh raspberries, blueberries, and mealworm pupae. She seized the cake, tasted it, and flung it. She picked individual drupelets off the raspberry, tasted each, and flung them, eating one. Chopped blueberries got the same treatment. While she was learning to pick up her own food, around Day 29, precious little was actually ingested. She trusted me, as she would trust a parent jay, to provide wholesome food, but caution ruled when she was on her own. This judiciousness is doubtless adaptive, especially since Jemima lacked jay companions from whom she could copy food selection. In everything the young jay did, I saw an overlay of intelligence that humbled me, and helped me realize that she would be going out into the world armed with common sense and a discriminating palate few would ascribe to a "gluttonous" blue jay.

Jemima considers several food options, arrayed on a doll plate sent by one of her fans. June 2.

Soaked dog kibble is the most frequently mentioned food for captive blue jays. It was one of the few things Jemima wouldn't touch. I got small sample bags of various brands of puppy and kitten chow at my local pet shop; all were rejected. I had hoped to get her eating a nutritious staple that, once she'd been released, the wild birds wouldn't bother with. So much for that plan! She occasionally ate a bit of chick starter, but never settled on any processed food as a staple. Mealworm pupae were always a hit, and I kept enough around in my basement bins so I could always find freshly molted tender white pupae. I'd pick them out first thing in the morning and refrigerate them to keep them tender as I doled them out to her throughout the day. Just another pro tip from a bird chef.

Mulberries were Jemima's favorite fruit, but her desire for fruit waned as she aged. The chopped blueberries, raspberries, watermelon, and cherries she'd cleaned up as a youngster went uneaten later. Fresh raw corn off the cob, shelled sugar snap peas from the garden, and a mixture of chopped sautéed chicken breast and rice continued to be popular. I supplemented the vegetables with raw pecans and walnuts and unsalted roasted peanuts. Salmon, pork, and rare filet were occasional treats that she eagerly gobbled. Was this jay spoiled? You bet. Jem was unabashedly spoiled, and eminently worth it.

I realize that it must sound as though I did nothing all day but observe, indulge, and cater to this young jay, and that case could be made. I did lots of other things as well. After a bit of adjustment, Jemima fit seamlessly into my everyday life, which already involved a lot of fussing around with fresh food for the humans under my care. When she was young and parked on her Easter basket in the kitchen, it was simple to work twice-hourly feedings into my routine, and it was no big deal to prepare little plates of fresh offerings for her once she started eating on her own. It was my honor to be her host. She gave me an excuse to stay home, be still, and watch, and home, still and watching, is the place I most love to be.

FOUR

Stuart

THE END OF May passed happily, with Jemima living mostly at large in the Big House, being banished to the flight tent only when there was no one to supervise her. At dusk on Day 24, she flew up from her perch on the back of the couch to the blades of a ceiling fan (which is very rarely used) and settled down to roost. I'd always caught her around dusk and put her in a pet carrier for the night, so she wouldn't go unsupervised should she awaken before me the next morning. Liam got her down by encouraging her to hop onto a broom, and we closed her in the carrier, but it was clear our bird was growing up, and her days in the cat carrier were numbered.

Do something already! Jemima's interactions with Stuart were decidedly one-sided.

Before she could fly well, Jemima spent most of her time on our kitchen chair backs. May 23.

Jemima was a joy to have in the house, as long as she wasn't pounding on Chet's toenails, poking into his ears, pulling yarn out of the hooked rugs, or pooping on upholstery and carpet. I kept small stacks of newspaper handy, so I could throw a sheet under whatever perch she'd selected. The house looked like a pet shop, but I told myself it was only for a little while, until she stopped taking syringe feedings and learned to eat from a dish. I slowed down and enjoyed her, and the precious time I had with her, knowing that it would be over too soon.

Jemima greeted our music, as well as the whirring microwave and churning dishwasher sounds, with enthusiastic song. I've noticed this behavior in other birds — canaries, pet budgies, and Charlie the macaw. They vocalized most when there was background noise as accompaniment. It seems to me they feel safe to sing out when others sing, too. Her song was much more complex and varied than one might expect from a corvid. It was based on low-pitched *burt* notes, interspersed with clicks, begging calls, scratchy noises, and an occasional *wooooeeeee??* that always made us laugh. There was something distinctly starling-like about the litany, which was spiked throughout with imitations of sounds that came too quickly to be identified. When we had to leave, or when Chet Baker had had enough pestering and we were forced to put Jemima in the fledging tent, she fell silent.

That is, until the day Phoebe heard what she thought was an adult jay insistently screaming the classic *JAY! JAY!* call, and realized it was coming from the garage. Worried, she ran closer until she could peek in the door. The moment Jemima spotted her, she fell silent again, but she wiped her bill, fluffed her feathers, and seemed particularly satisfied that her SOS had magically produced her favorite person. She had found her voice on Day 25. From this day on, it was obvious when Jemima had had enough of solitary confinement, and someone usually went to rescue her. We carried her from the garage to the house cradled in our hands. We couldn't risk her getting loose outdoors until she was reliably self-feeding. We were caught between encouraging her independence by leaving her alone, and the fact that she moped and refused to eat when left by herself. Jemima solved that problem in fine jay style — by yelling orders.

I was still thinking about the problem of imprinting, which is a gray area for corvids. An imprinted bird identifies as a human and may never socialize properly with its own kind.

When Jemima's toenail pounding and ear probing became onerous, Chet Baker appreciated a drape. June 14.

I'd read that if a jay is fully feathered when taken in by humans — that is, if it has had vital early contact with others of its species — it should identify as a jay and not a person, selecting a species-appropriate mate when the time came. Jemima, by my guess, was perhaps eleven days old when she tumbled from her nest. She was fully feathered, if tailless and stub-winged. Whether she'd had enough early experience with her parents to grow up believing she was a jay remained to be seen.

Though Jemima had been parent raised until Day 11, I was concerned enough about the specter of imprinting to put out a word to the Ohio Wildlife Center that I was interested in raising another young jay as a companion for her. By May 23, a fledgling jay had come into the clinic, and I drove to Athens to meet Connie, the OWC volunteer who'd been caring for it.

Stuart, a companion for Jemima, arrived in a softly padded plastic cup. May 25.

Beautifully feathered, the youngster lay quietly in a padded cup. It gaped soundlessly for food, perhaps a bit overwhelmed by the artificial environment and changing cast of caretakers. When I gathered it into my hands, I was struck by the heat coming off the bird. Its abdomen was soft, swollen. That, I knew, was abnormal. There was something not right about this bird. I took it home and started it on the wide-spec-

From the beginning, Jemima loudly solicited Stuart's attention.

trum antibiotic Baytril. I designated a feeding syringe and water dropper just for the new bird, in case its illness was contagious. Rats, rats, rats. I had hoped for a healthy bird, and this one looked beautiful, ate well, and produced normal droppings. By its size and feathering, it was easily seventeen days old, and I knew it should have fledged by now. Yet it sat still day after day, seemingly unwilling or unable to hop or flutter.

Jemima was instantly intrigued by the bird, whom I named Stuart, for the mnemonic of a common call of blue jays. We settled on male for his sex, knowing we had a 50 percent chance of being correct. Jemima approached our new charge again and again, mouth agape, wings fluttering, keening. It wasn't begging behavior, exactly; it was more importuning. When Stuart failed to hop out of his nest and join her, Jemima began to peck him, even tugging on his wing feathers, in a seeming effort to goad him into action. While she clambered around on my drawing table and fluttered atop my swing-arm lamp, Stuart stayed put. I continued feeding him, wondering if antibiotics and good food could bring him around. By May 27, I was taking Stuart out of the nest and encouraging him to hop and move. He was quite a bit brighter, more interested in his surroundings, but sitting stock-still. He couldn't hop; he couldn't do much more than sit back on his hocks and watch the world moving around him. When he tried to preen, he'd topple over sideways. My vision of the two exploring the house and later the fledging tent and the world outside as a duo was beginning to crumble. Jemima hopped circles around him and had to be closely supervised lest her light pecks devolve to pounding. Pounding on things is what blue jays do.

By May 29, it was clear to me that Stuart was not just unwilling, but unable to move. A twenty-three-day-old jay should be bouncing off the walls. I called in support from Dr. Robert F. Giddings, board-certified avian veterinarian and old friend from my Connecticut days. I described Stuart's warm, swollen hock and foot joints, his inactivity, and the distended abdomen that concerned me. Bob told me to check his wing joints for swelling. I was distressed to find heat and swelling in them as well. Bob opined that Stuart had an infection in his blood, which had likely been contracted through the eggshell membrane — he'd probably been born with it. The distended, warm abdomen was a sign of peritonitis. Baytril would be the antibiotic of choice, but the likelihood of curing the infection was small, given that Stuart hadn't responded to a week of treatment. More importantly, the chronic swelling and inflammation in his joints had likely damaged them to the point that they'd be unusable for locomotion and the delicate maneuvers of flight. In a flash, I understood that Stuart hadn't left the nest simply because he couldn't. He had been in pain the whole time. And I knew, given the prognosis Bob had sketched out, what I had to do.

I told Liam and Phoebe what I'd learned, and neither was surprised, for they'd sensed that Stuart was compromised from the start. Liam, our court jester, had referred to him from the start as our "sickly Victorian child," and spoken for Stuart in a comically effete voice. "Stop pounding on me, Jemima, and make yourself useful. Bring me another crumpet, for I cahn't get out of bed." Kids know things, often before their parents do. If I'm grateful for anything, it's that my kids have participated in my work with birds, and they've known from an early age that not all creatures we take in are destined to make it. More than that, they understand that to be releasable, a bird must be all but perfect. I asked that Phoebe and Liam say their goodbyes to Stuart while I was away. I suited up and took a four-mile run, culminating in a hard climb to the top of a high hayfield. I breathed deeply and asked why it had to be this way. The gray-bellied clouds drifting overhead didn't reply.

Euthanizing a living creature is the hardest thing I have to do as a rehabilitator. Living far out in the country and working with wildlife, I'm regularly presented with difficult situations that can't be shunted off to someone else. Teaching myself to deal with death — and to deal it — has been a necessary evil, because death is always part of the picture when you are trying to save small lives. My home isn't a hospital, and I don't have a medicine cabinet stocked with injectable drugs. All I have is my

Stuart's swollen joints and feet bespoke a grave prognosis. May 28.

two hands, and a heart that breaks each time I have to use them to take a life. The clinical, white-coated term is "cervical dislocation"; the country words are "wringing its neck." I kissed Stuart on his dear head, breathed in his scent one last time, apologized, and swiftly sent him off to the next world.

I looked down at my hands: work-worn, squarish; capable of infinite gentleness and a soothing, healing touch, but when necessary, also capable of dealing swift release from suffering. It's a rotten thing to have to do. I'm never the same afterward. I'm sadder and wiser, and I know a little bit more about what you can fix and what you can't. I suppose that's a good thing. But there's a piece of me that breaks off and flies away with a bird like Stuart, and I'm not sure it ever comes back.

FIVE

Life with Jemima

THE PRESENCE OF a single bird can change everything for one who appreciates them. Imagine a quiet, east-facing woodland slope on a May morning. Backlit leaves shuffle and twinkle in the breeze. Suddenly you spot a worm-eating warbler dangling head-down as it searches for insects, hidden in the dead-leaf clusters. It's a subtly bewitching shade of ochre green, with deep chocolate stripes on its crown. Its strong, sharp-pointed bill opens wide as it pries into curled leaves, looking for spiders. All your senses zero in on that busy little bird. Your world contracts to the small circle of your binocular view. When you finally bring the binoculars down, inhale, and look around, the

---

I kept feeders stocked with peanuts to encourage visits by wild jays. Jemima watched by the hour from her kitchen chair. Their soft conversation floated in the open casement window.

wooded slope has changed. It is no longer bland and feature-less. For you, it will forever be worm-eating warbler habitat, the presence of that tiny bird transforming the place entirely.

The presence of a small gray-blue puff of feathers transformed our home, too. A kitchen is a different place when there's a jay ensconced on the back of a chair, the dark beads of its eyes following your every move. Working at the drafting table for hours at a time is a different pursuit when there's a snooty-looking baby jay sitting on the swing-arm lamp, a syringe of nestling formula within easy reach. Jemima had been incorporated into the house and our lives. We walked nowhere without checking to see if she was hopping across the floor in front of us. I gave a rueful smile each time I walked into the newspaper-festooned kitchen, saw the inelegant sheet covering the sofa. *It's only for a little while longer, just until we can release her . . .*

For raising a jay is not like raising other songbirds. Jays are intensely social beings. They do almost nothing alone. Wherever they go, they arrive and leave together. The jay flocks, as small as five to as many as thirteen, who winter on our sanctuary come sweeping in on a November cold front and brighten my life until they depart in April. Although it was sometimes

A kitchen busy with life: pot pie ingredients and feeding syringe on the table, Chet snuffling hopefully, Jemima surveying from the chair back.

frustrating to see them plop down and vacuum up seed until their throat pouches bulged, the fanfare of cobalt and white as they whirled away with the booty made it all worthwhile, even before I fixated on blue jays. I've always been happy to buy enough seed and cracked corn for everyone.

It was a stroke of great good fortune that Phoebe was home for Jemima's early weeks. She took Jemima's socialization seriously, knowing that, imperfect as it was, our family was Jemima's flock. And the little jay was never far from Phoebe, Liam, or me, always ready for a conversation. Phoebe played song after song on her iPhone, lying on the floor, nose to bill. Jemima seemed to love these song sessions, raising her crest, extending her neck, and singing in a sweet cascade of *burt burt burt* notes, interspersed with clicks, gurgles, screeling wails, and scratchy staccato notes. She seemed sensitive to the dynamics of each song, extending her wings and singing more loudly at the crescendos so typical of country songs. Phoebe said that Jemima's tastes ran to newer country and Ed Sheeran; oddly enough, so do hers. It was clear even to a casual observer that Sheeran's bouncy "Barcelona" elicited the greatest response from Jemima, and it became a signature sound of our home in the weeks before Jemima's release.

As I watched the young jay interacting with people and our Boston terrier, Chet Baker, I sometimes thought about whooping cranes and condors, to name just two endangered species that have been pulled from the brink of extinction by extreme human intervention. I thought about the great lengths to which people go to try to avoid imprinting in these endangered birds. Imprinting is defined by Merriam-Webster as "a rapid learning process that takes place early in the life of a social animal (as a goose) and establishes a behavior pattern (as recognition of and attraction to its own kind or a substitute)."

Our last outdoor photo shoot before Jemima began to fly. May 23.

Imprinting is a survival tactic that sends just-hatched ducks swimming after the mother duck and, we hope, not an otter.

It's that "substitute" option, always out there, that haunts the human caretakers of birds prone to imprinting. Thanks to their sociality, jays and other corvids fall into this group. But imagine having a four-foot-tall, fifteen-pound, critically endangered bird with a life expectancy nudging forty years decide that you're her forever love. This happened to George Archibald with a whooping crane named Tex, and he wound up dancing energetically with her in the spring, having her artificially inseminated, and collecting her eggs for captive propagation of this vanishing species. He also cofounded the International Crane Foundation; whether his first dances with Tex and the eventual formation of a crane conservation organization are connected is hardly open to question. One does what one must.

Hoping to avoid such a scenario, human stewards of hand-raised whooping crane chicks don elaborate crane costumes, hunched under a white sheet, with a papier-mâché crane head held aloft on one arm, like a puppet. California condor chicks are kept for hand-raising in a box, behind one-way glass, and fed from the beak of a condor hand puppet that appears from a hole in the back. I have always wondered whether these well-intentioned ruses actually fool the young birds. Birds, after all, are masters of observation. Shouldn't a condor, a scavenger whose living would depend on it, be able to tell unerringly if something is alive or not? I realize that the people charged with raising the birds are adhering to scientific theory and doing the best they can. But a life spent raising songbirds, and continually being surprised at their powers of perception, leaves me wondering if the birds really buy into the illusion.

I recall walking into the living room wearing a monster mask that covered my entire head, just to see what my chestnut-fronted macaw, Charlie, might do. Charlie, who was notoriously wary and aggressive toward strangers, greeted me with her usual happy conversational sounds, ran up my arm to my shoulder, and began to tug at the mask. There was no doubt from her reaction that she recognized everything else about me and wanted to see Julie underneath the latex. Having heard stories about pet cockatoos who freaked out and fell to pieces when their owners dyed their hair or simply came out of the shower with a towel on their heads, I was impressed. On another occasion, I launched a ten-inch-long battery-powered toy tarantula across the studio floor. Charlie was extremely wary of spiders, wasps — anything that might have a sting or bite. She'd give such insects a wide berth, making little stabbing feints that showed she was cognizant of what they might do. Faced with a toy spider as large as she was, Charlie's pupils pinned to dots, and she quickly waddled up to the enormous, slowly crawling thing, grabbed it by the thorax, and flipped it upside down without the slightest sign of fear. She gave a human *Ha HAAA!!* and did a little pigeon-toed dance of victory as its legs swam helplessly in the air. I believe Charlie had a finely honed concept of "alive" versus "inanimate."

As a social creature, Jemima was hardwired to keep company with other living creatures. She had a relationship with Chet Baker that was odd, touching, a bit concerning, and often hilarious. Chet went about all his business with a hopping, nattering escort. Jemima fluttered her wings and gave insistent begging calls as she dogged his every move. This was, in fact, female solicitation, a hard indicator of her sex. Several times, he tripped over her or even stepped on her; Jem would give a loud, indignant squawk, pick herself up, and continue her pursuit. She was a tough little bird. In his twilight year, Chet spent a lot of his day napping, and Jemima would seize this opportunity to poke her beak into his ears and between his toes. She'd insert her bill, then open her mandibles to spread his toes apart, and pound on his nails with ever-increasing force. (Blue jays pound on the ones they love.) Chet's response was to flinch, pull his paws closer to his body, and close his eyes again. When she persisted, he'd sigh, get up, walk a short distance away, and flop down again. And the chase would go on.

Chet was a good, good dog. Ever since he was the age of nine weeks, I'd given him to understand that birds were never to be harmed. When he was too young to walk through the tall grass, I carried him on my shoulder through the meadow as I checked our bluebird nest boxes. I allowed him to sniff the eggs and young chicks, while murmuring to him to leave them alone. Boston terriers are extremely sensitive to tone of voice, and I found I could control his interactions with the birds just by speaking softly to him. This training and habituation to the scent and presence of birds was vital if I was to raise orphaned songbirds in his presence, and it was remarkably effective. Presented with a nestling, Chet would sniff it briefly, then refuse

Just checkin' the oil, sir.

to look directly at it ever again. His mien suggested that he wanted to resist at all costs the temptation to grab it.

Chet's ability to tell a bird from a mammal was sorely tested in mid-October 2008. I was hanging clothes on the line when a small, brown, hunchbacked creature came running toward me from the shrubbery around our small water garden, Chet in hot pursuit. I thought at first it was a young rabbit as it made a beeline right toward me. Pressed hard, the creature opened and flapped its wings as it ran, and four-year-old Chet slammed on the brakes and sat down to watch it dive behind a hose reel. He'd mistaken a Virginia rail — a species never recorded before or since on our dry ridgetop — for a small mammal and didn't realize his error until he saw it flutter. Neither, for that matter, did I. Rails on the run resemble nothing so much as rodents. My heart burst with pride for my little dog who, even in the heat of the moment, knew wings when he saw them.

When Phoebe and Liam, aged thirteen and ten, pestered

me long enough to break down and buy them a pair of Chinese dwarf hamsters, I was more than a little apprehensive about controlling Chet Baker's prey drive. For though he would never harm a bird under his nose, he was hell on chipmunks, squirrels, and rabbits. Sure enough, Chet would sit by the hour, trembling slightly, a bubble of drool forming at the corner of his jowls, watching the hamsters' every move within the safety of their covered tank. More than once we came into the room to find him shoving the tank with his paws, doubtless hoping to overturn it. Once, Chet left the ground from a sitting position, helicoptering straight up to try to snatch a hamster that Liam was holding under his chin. When the hamsters finally got old and doddery and then expired, we all breathed a sigh of relief, resolving never to own small mammals again.

This dog, unreliable around small furry animals, was a perfect gentleman with Jemima. It was she who was the heathen, the insufferable pest, forever trying to elicit some kind of response from kind, stoic Chet. He'd look up at me with his

Please. Do something with this infernal bird.

big, world-weary eyes, imploring me to intercede on his behalf. There were days when Jemima was so persistent in pounding on his toes and tweaking his ears and tail that I'd lean down, gently capture her, and take her out to her tent in the garage for a few hours' time-out, to give Chet a chance to nap undisturbed.

It seemed to me that Jemima, robbed by circumstance of her jay siblings and parents, had selected, in Chet Baker, the closest thing to a bird that she could find. I believe she was forced to settle for and zero in on the only other nonhuman in the place. I could see that she was frustrated by his inappropriate response to her overtures, just as she'd been stymied by poor Stuart, who couldn't join her in tearing up bouquets and flying around the living room. Just as she'd pestered Stuart, she was always after Chet. She'd squeal louder and pound harder on Chet's toenails when she failed to get a satisfactory outcome. He was clearly annoyed by this, but sweet Baker was a gentleman through and through. I was thankful that Phoebe and Liam were both home to sing and play with Jemima, to lavish affection and stimulation on a bird who seemed to badly need it.

In hopes that they'd become Jemima's new social unit, I spent the summer of 2017 closely observing the jay family resident in our yard. I'd been lucky enough to photograph the male feeding the female on May 11, when she was in the midst of nest construction and egg laying. My photographs show the female, her breast wet and dirty from nest construction, being fed by a well-marked, immaculate male. In jay pairs, the male feeds the female, not the other way around. I felt lucky to have photographed this event, and to find plumage markers that would allow me to distinguish them from each other through the summer. Blackbelt and Jayne would bring two juveniles to the feeders all summer long. Their family ties were strong; the

Blackbelt, right, feeds his mate Jayne, left. Her breast is wet and soiled from nest building. It's possible to sex jays only when you catch them doing something like this—that is, it's practically impossible.

young birds always arrived, traveled, fed, and departed with at least one parent, and I could hear the young jays begging and being fed long after they were visually almost indistinguishable from their parents. Only one parent and one youngster came to the feeder at a time for the first several weeks. After this period, the two juveniles often arrived with both parents in a group of four. Their togetherness seemed as much a social behavior as it was a survival tactic, and it impressed me deeply that the blue jay is a bird that invests heavily — for months, in fact — in the education and acculturation of its young. As it unfolded, one of the pair's two young would go on to play an important role in Jemima's life.

We did what we could to assure that Jemima knew she was a jay. She sat by the hour at the kitchen table, watching jays come and go from the feeder just outside. I put out peanuts to attract them where Jemima could watch. When a jay arrived, her crown feathers would flatten, then raise; she'd give the bird her full attention for as long as it was in sight. When I played blue jay calls on my laptop, she was galvanized and rapt, looking about for danger when alarm calls were played, and cocking

her head thoughtfully for whisper song playback. Jay vocalizations clearly held meaning for her, as did the sight of the jays
themselves.

A video I watched, of blue jay fledglings being hand-
reared at a wildlife rehabilitation center, haunts me. The birds
were confined together in a cage that was covered by a cloth,
keeping them in half-darkness. At feeding time, the cloth was
briefly lifted, and food stuffed into each gaping mouth. Then
the cloth was replaced. The birds saw nothing more, received
no more contact than was necessary to keep them alive. The
caretakers in such facilities are under strict orders to not speak
to the birds or interact with them other than to feed them. The
concept seems to be to keep contact with humans at an absolute minimum, to preserve the self-image of the fledglings as
jays and not humans. In the parlance of orthodox wildlife rehabilitators, any more contact, including touch and speaking to
one's charge, constitutes "bunny hugging," and is strongly dis-
couraged, with the specter of imprinting held up as the care-
taker's ultimate failure.

The contrast between this treatment and Jemima's busy
and enriched environment could not be more drastic or stark.
I have to wonder how birds raised in such isolation and free
of outside stimulus and early exercise would fare upon release.
Yes, they've seen other young jays. They've been stuffed full of
food and left to their own devices in isolation. They've seen
their human caretakers in brief flashes, and without question
have learned to connect them with the sudden, if clinical, pro-
vision of food. But have they had a chance to play Jungle Jem?
Polish their vocal chops singing along to Ed Sheeran? Bathe in
a pie plate and dry off, preening in the sun? Fly from room to
room searching for company? Watch adult jays at the feeder?
Pester an old dog? Catch a roach sneaking along the baseboard?

We did what we could to keep Jemima active and engaged, and that turned out to be a lot. Whenever I was gripped with uncertainty about whether I was doing right by Jemima, I remembered that without us she'd be dead, and led with my heart. My heart told me this bird needed to be part of a family, however imperfect, and she'd sort out where she fit in the species spectrum as she went along. I had a hunch that, since she was eleven days old and feathered out upon intake, she had had the critical early visual and aural experience to let her identify as a jay. In the meantime, we'd give her the best family we could — full of music and laughter, exercise and play, new foods and new situations, with the security of our constant presence as big lumpy featherless jay-parent substitutes. If that meant I didn't go much of anywhere for a couple of months, if our dog lost some sleep and our house was spattered with whitewash, so be it. This bird would grow up strong, engaged, and circled in love.

SIX

Release

BY THE FIRST week of June, Jemima was a real handful in the house. She followed Chet Baker tirelessly, chittering, fluttering, and crisscrossing under his belly as he walked. She took advantage of his naps to perch and preen on his back, and good, sweet Chet barely flinched anymore when she landed on him in full flight. She delighted in sorting through Liam's multicolored markers and colored pencils, knocking over the action figures he used for models for his vivid anime art, and pounding the erasers off his mechanical pencils. I was grateful that she had yet to display the penchant for thievery for which blue jays and crows are famous, for she spent hours in my studio.

Release! The infinite expansion of Jemima's world found her wary and hanging close to the house at first.

Action figures, and their tiny plastic pieces, are tailor-made for thieving jays.
May 30.

By early June, she was flying from kitchen to living room to studio, even up and down long flights of stairs. She discovered the wall-length mirror in the master bathroom and loved to fly down the dark stairwell to see what that downstairs jay was up to. She'd then spend some time throwing coins and jewelry off a bedroom dresser and hopping across the quilt as if it were a big trampoline. She flew to the chandelier in the foyer and from there through a cutout in the wall and up two flights of steps to our glassed-in tower room. From there, she could command a view of the whole yard. Jemima had plumbed the heights and depths of our house, showing an impressive command of flight in confined spaces. Release time was near. Once she was picking up all her own food and no longer taking hand-feedings, she'd be released.

Before dawn on June 7, Phoebe was packed to start her trip back to Maine for her summer job on Bowdoin's campus. Though I would have loved to go along to drop her at the airport in Columbus, I stayed home with Jemima, who was still taking syringe feedings and needed constant supervision in the house. I couldn't imagine leaving her in the garage tent all day. It was ironic that caring for this bird had prevented me from both picking up and delivering my daughter for her summer break, but Phoebe understood that this deep, yet fleeting commitment was one to be honored. She had drunk in every minute of the experience of raising Jemima, pouring love and attention into a small blue vial. But now it was time to part.

Phoebe had one last song session with Jemima before daybreak, breathing in her birdy scent and hoping hard the little jay would still be around when she came home again in late August. Jemima sang lustily, waving her wings and turning up her scratchy tune at "Barcelona's" crescendo. My misty-eyed daughter sang along. I saw her soaking up the magic of this bird, trying to save it for the times when she'd miss Jemima. My kids have had many such goodbyes with their temporary wild companions, and they don't get any easier. Finally, it was time to leave. My little family rolled away down the drive, and the house was quiet. I marveled at how completely I'd been subsumed in the role of bird mother, at the perfection of having something that demanded attention just as my children were making their own way into the world. My maternal instincts, always strong, were being channeled by circumstance into a bird, as I resolved to see this jay's upbringing through, to whatever outcome awaited.

Jemima looks out on a downpour from the comfort of my swing-arm lamp in the studio. May 31.

Phoebe soaks up a little Jemima before she leaves for her summer work in Maine. June 6.

Jem was perched on the back of my drafting stool later that morning when a male rose-breasted grosbeak who'd been visiting the feeders came into the evergreen just outside the studio window. It perched only a yard away, eyeing Jemima curiously. She took immediate interest, raising and flattening her crest, bowing, shuffling her wings, and spreading her tail. For more than a minute, she flew back and forth in front of the window, making eye contact with the grosbeak the whole time. *Sturrt! Sturrt!* she called. The rose-breast fixed first one eye, then the other on this odd bird, seeming to wonder why it was inside a house with the woman who fills the feeders. I yearned to open the window and let Jemima out to meet this curious bird, but she needed just a few more days to become independent. Soon enough, Jem.

Jemima was taking daily baths at this point, in a Pyrex pie plate we kept on the kitchen floor. She'd soak herself beyond recognition, then hop soggily up to a chair back to preen dry in the sun. I worried about the way her feathers would become waterlogged with the first dip and shuffle in the water. She could no more fly when saturated than I could, and that

situation might prove dangerous once she was in the wild. I remembered this issue with other birds I'd hand-raised and wondered if the seeming lack of natural oils in her plumage could be
linked to a dietary deficiency. I started looking more closely at
the birds in my yard, especially on rainy days, and noticed that
juveniles as a rule had poor waterproofing. Juvenal plumage is
looser, fluffier, and not as tight to the body as adult plumage,
and this fluffy nature, with less efficient "zipping together" of
the barbicels, contributes to its absorbency. Hoping that daily
or twice-daily baths would encourage preening and spreading
of Jemima's natural oils, I kept a pie plate on hand for Jemima.

I handed Jem her first peanut, a cocktail half, when she
was thirty-five days old. I could see all the lights on her mental
switchboard coming on as she hopped and fluttered around the
studio looking for a place to either hide or process it. She held it
briefly in her toes, dropped it, recovered it, and took it for a ride

A wild rose-breasted grosbeak peers curiously at the blue jay in the studio.
June 7.

around the room for the better part of an hour. If she was going to be inefficient and preoccupied, it was best she do that in the safety of the house. It would be at least two more weeks before she was able to perch and pound a peanut into edible bits while holding it in her toes. Watching her slowly master the neurological pathways to this feat was fascinating. There's a lot a jay needs to learn to function and feed.

Exploring peanuts produced an uptick in her interest in diverse foods. By June 9, the kitchen table was a culinary playground. She landed on my salad bowl, picked out leaves of spring mix, and shook and thrashed them as if they were winged insects. She dissected tomatoes and picked at Parmesan. A serving bowl of watermelon was suddenly adorned with a full-sized jay who stabbed a chunk, tossed it back into her throat pouch, then took off for the living room couch, where she searched for a place to cache it. Liam shook his head, watching. I cackled as I followed her around the room, marveling at my own stretchy tolerance for such mayhem in my house. It was all about the jay now. My mother would definitely not have approved. Jemima gave me a fascinating glimpse into the developing mind of a bird, and no stain or mess could dim my delight at seeing her grow up to fulfill her birthright as a thief and miscreant.

It's a joy to write Jemima's story, because I have recorded it all so thoroughly in photos and videos. A two-minute clip from June 10 has her perched on my drafting table lamp, singing her heart out to "Barcelona," swinging to the happy beat, taken away by the music coming from the speakers and her pulsing throat. I thought back to her early days, hopping stubtailed across the floor. Same song, different bird. Her tail was full-length; her shiny black bill was thick and strong, and she flew powerfully on wide blue wings. She would spend her last night in the pet carrier tonight.

Jemima stalled her own release with a soaking bath, grounding herself for another two hours. June 11.

June 11 would be Release Day. Jemima was thirty-eight days old. I got up early to fix her last breakfast in the fledging tent. She was finally taking all her food from the dish, whether I was present or not. I photographed the plate, smiling as it occurred to me that it was something like a convict's last meal before hitting the street in civilian clothes. Tender white mealworms, chopped strawberries, blueberries, raspberries, sweet corn, mulberries, and cornbread — what a spread for an omnivorous bird! I was proud that Jemima had avoided the culinary tunnel vision so common in captive birds, that she was willing to try anything new that appeared on her plate. I took her in her night carrier to the tent and instead of offering her a syringe of formula, simply opened the carrier and showed her the plate. Just outside the tent, an ovenbird and a field sparrow sang, and the insistent calls of a jay rang out as Jemima tossed back her deluxe breakfast. I knew, from so many previous release events, that this was not the end of Jemima's story, but an exciting beginning. The birds were singing her home.

I left Jemima to her breakfast and took a slow jog with

Chet Baker on this glorious blue and green June morning. It got my blood going and my lungs working. I'd need a clear head to go through with the release of this precious being, who'd brightened all our lives for almost a month now. I'd gone to the grocery store and laid in food for a week, because I knew I would be spending a lot of time outside with Jemima in the days to come. I didn't want to have to go anywhere, didn't want to miss a thing. I returned to the tent, intending to bring her out under the open sky, only to find Jem taking a twenty-second bath in her pie plate that left her saturated. It would be another hour and a half before she'd be dry enough for release. I came back to the tent and talked softly to her for a moment, then gently cupped my hands around her and carried her outside. Liam and Bill were waiting under the Japanese maple in whose branches I'd rigged up a small wooden shelf for her food and water dishes. It was the same tree where I'd found the jay nest and the egg that started it all. I'd been thinking about this day for a long time.

It felt so very odd to close my fingers around Jemima and carry her in my hands, as I had for weeks, taking her from the

The moment of release, June 11. The small platform is her feeding station. The Japanese maple would be home base for her. (Bill Thompson III)

Chet Baker was a comforting presence for the newly free blue jay. June 11.

garage to the house, knowing that this time I would open them and release her into the verdure outside. I walked with her, wide-eyed and struggling a little, to the maple, and showed her the shelf with food and water. Then I opened my hands. She hopped to a branch, then to another. She fluffed her feathers and shook them out. She spied an ant running up the trunk, grabbed it and crushed it in her bill, then swallowed it. Her first wild prey! I showed her the food and water dishes, then replaced them on the little shelf. Jemima would spend the rest of the afternoon perched quietly in the maple. I sat in a lawn chair just beneath, giving her the security of my presence, so she never felt abandoned. Lacking wings to fly with her, it was the best I could do. In the first two hours, she'd visit her food dishes eight times, eating avidly. She'd also land at my feet, grabbing Japanese beetles out of the grass and crunching them down. She seemed to want to learn all she could about this home base I'd made for her before venturing any farther afield. I'd never had a bird handle its release so conservatively, so wisely. Her corvid sociality tied her to me, even as her flexible mind gave her foraging tools and the curiosity to employ them.

When Jemima finally widened her sphere, she headed for the evergreen by the front door and set up camp in its shelter. I rigged up another feeding station there, a little basket with food and water, tied in the tree. She came down to use it within minutes. The weather had turned hot, and I'd put Jemima's pie plate bathtub out for her in a planter nearby. Late that afternoon, she descended for a bath, soaking herself as usual. She attempted to fly up to a perch and landed on the ground with a plop, looking stricken. She seemed to realize the peril she'd put herself in and scuttled like a frightened rat under a boxwood. I captured her and brought her in the house to preen herself dry

On the hunt for pillbugs in a new world, rich with potential. June 12.

in the kitchen. Yes, she'd been released, but that didn't mean she had to stay outside around the clock. She was allowed a mistake or two, especially with her protector standing by.

Evening fell, and I decided to keep her inside for the night. She flew up to a high perch in the studio, fluffed her feathers, preened, and settled down for a night's sleep after an eventful day. For tonight at least, she'd be safe from things that climb, fly, grab, and go hoot in the night. I exhaled and smiled up at this bird of growing expertise and nascent good sense. We'd take this release slowly, letting her live between two worlds as long as she needed to.

SEVEN

Titmouse Wars

FOR THE NEXT week after Jemima's release, I spent a lot of time outside writing in the shade of the Japanese maple, my binoculars and camera at hand. This served a dual purpose. I could be alert to anything happening in Jemima's new, expanded outdoor world, and I could keep the dang titmice off her food dishes in the tree just over my head.

In 1992, when Bill and I first moved to the eighty-acre property we'd name Indigo Hill, the local birds were naïve. There were no bird feeders within two miles of our home, and I remember waiting weeks before the first bird landed on the tube feeder we'd hung off the deck. That first bird was a tufted

Pirates at the secret studio feeder. Local residents were quick to take advantage of Jemima's buffet.

titmouse, intelligent innovator, pioneer of plasticity, able to mold its behavior to the situation at hand. Now, twenty-five years later, the local bird population is completely attuned to the amenities offered here, from peanut and suet feeders to thistle and sunflower tubes. It took the tufted titmice two days to discover Jemima's special feeding stations in the Japanese maple and the tall evergreen by the door, and just minutes to empty them. More than just an annoyance, the titmouse piracy compromised my ability to provide for Jemima in the tenuous period while she was learning how to find food for herself.

When raising and releasing two orphaned bluebirds in Connecticut in the mid-1980s, I'd been frustrated by a gray catbird who emptied their mealworm dish as soon as I filled it. I suspected that the thief was the catbird I'd raised and released the summer before — well acquainted with me and my ways and primed to exploit the situation. I solved that problem by figuring out a food delivery system that would work for bluebirds but not for a catbird. I trained the orphans to enter a small plastic hamster house for their food. Being cavity nesters, bluebirds are naturally curious and willing to poke their heads inside a hole. Entering a box is outside the pale for a catbird. In

July 5's brunch menu: broiled salmon and garden-fresh snap peas.

Is it any wonder Jemima kept returning? Having gorged on chicken, rice, and fresh sweet corn, a well-fed Jemima selects a pecan to carry off and cache.

this way, I was able to deliver food to the bluebirds I'd worked so hard to raise, and only to them.

I knew I had to solve this new dilemma quickly, to keep the unbroken food supply going. It was June 13, and Jemima had been released only two days earlier. She was by no means ready for complete independence. I decided to train Jemima to come in to eat at the crank-out window in my studio. At first, I called her to me and fed her by holding the dishes in my hand out the studio window. When she keyed in to the location, I made a small platform there as a feeding tray. This worked well for several days. When the titmice found it and began to empty the dishes, I tied a small shallow basket under the rooflike shelter of the crank-out window and put Jem's food cups in it. Jemima passed under the window without hesitation, but the titmice were leery of such confines. Of course, the delicious repast offered there soon conquered the wild birds' fear, and the piracy continued. What's a little inconvenience when there are mealworms waiting? A hairy woodpecker joined in, and within days, I had trouble keeping enough food there for Jemima. This was getting ridiculous. It was the downside of having catered to the yard birds' every need for a couple of decades. They figured everything I provided was meant for them.

Feeling more than a little foolish, I decided to try some aversive conditioning. I was attuned to the scratchy sound of bird toenails on the basket behind my back as I worked at my drawing table. "*BLAAAA!*" I'd blurt, and lunge at the titmice when they arrived. They got used to that, too, and made their raids even more stealthily, watching to make sure I was gone or deeply absorbed in something before approaching. Time to escalate. Picturing myself as Wile E. Coyote opening his latest box from Acme, I filled a spray bottle with water and set the nozzle to issue a jet stream. I had several out-of-body experiences as I watched myself sitting at the drawing table, tense as a cat, waiting for a pirate titmouse to land so I could try to hit it with a well-aimed squirt to the face. One experience was enough for the hairy woodpecker, who panicked, blundered around in the basket, found her way back out, and never returned. I felt bad about that, as my ferocious desire to feed my foundling jay drove me to new behavioral lows.

The titmice were another matter: just as adaptable to squirt aversion treatment as they were to scare tactics. I have to say that, awful as it is, there is not much that's more fun than trying to hit a titmouse with a squirt bottle. I suppose it offered the same sort of stimulus to me that video games or skeet shooting might, if I were ever so inclined. The titmice were completely unfazed and kept cleaning out the mealworms and pecans as if getting squirted in the face were just a part of the quirky service at this dive. Once again, I had to concede defeat, a big dumb Wile E. Coyote with a pack of five tiny gray roadrunners besting me at every turn.

I was outnumbered, and the titmice had long since stopped taking me seriously. I felt like a perfect fool. Over the

A juvenile tufted titmouse, one of five who bedeviled me by helping themselves to Jemima's food. It even looks bratty.

ensuing months, I arrived at a shaky equilibrium with the dang titmice, who were soon joined at the "secret" studio feeder by cardinals, American goldfinches, house finches, and Carolina wrens. I bought the wild birds off with sunflower hearts, offered at the far end of the basket feeder, and kept Jemima fed with a mix of cooked chicken, brown rice, and sweet corn at the end nearest my drawing table. The spooky wild birds could fill up at the far end, while the tame hand-raised one had to hop a couple of feet under the overhanging window (and closer to me) to get her treat. Save for a couple of titmice and a Carolina wren who developed a taste for chicken and sweet corn, the wild birds were mostly satisfied to stuff themselves on sunflower hearts and dash away. Jemima was willing to hop farther under the windowpane and that much closer to me for her special food, which wasn't as attractive to the wild birds. I'd put a few pecan halves out whenever she was around and watching; at sixteen dollars per pound, I wasn't interested in supplying the neighborhood titmice with such fare. It was a humbling lesson to be so thoroughly outwitted and exploited by titmice, whose three-quarter-ounce weight, I'm convinced, consists mostly of brass and brains.

EIGHT

Vigilance and Intelligence

THE MID-JUNE DAYS rolled forward with Jemima spending most of her time outdoors. Heat, haze, and humidity settled in. After her experience getting soaked and losing her powers of flight in the outdoor bath, Jemima was wary of bathing. It was just another lesson in survival that she had to learn through a mistake. Being a corvid, brainy and innovative, Jemima came to a novel solution for the problem. For several days running, she came to the front door and screamed as the sun climbed high in the hazy sky. *Jay! Jay! Jay!* Ever the faithful servant, I'd hurry to see what she wanted. When I'd open the screen door, Jemima would fly into the foyer and straight to Chet Baker's water bowl

Jemima had never seen a snake, but her preprogrammed alarm system worked perfectly.

in the kitchen. Plop! She'd leap in and get herself thoroughly saturated, then flutter up to the back of a kitchen chair to preen in the sun, safe from predators in the friendly confines of her house. I marveled at the way she made her desire clear and exploited the situation to her advantage. And I loved having her home for a few hours.

After one misstep outside, Jemima realized that the soaking baths she loved had to be taken in the safety of the house. Here, she's just emerged from Chet's water bowl on a broiling hot June 14.

Along the way, as I shared stories and photos of Jemima learning to be a wild bird with the generous subsidy of food and occasional shelter, some people questioned how Jemima would learn vigilance behavior without wild parents to teach her about danger. It was a fair question. I thought back to an American robin I'd raised years earlier. Its release was particularly dicey, thanks to a rambunctious black Labrador belonging to my landlords. The robin had never been exposed to predators, and, oddly, it seemed to lack a template for recognizing the danger this dog presented. I remember sprinting to tackle Derry as she'd charge the young robin, which held its ground even as the dog headed toward it. I'd give my best imitation of the robin's *Keep! Keep! Keep!* alarm call and rush at the bird, waving my arms, trying to force it to fly at the first sight of this murderous animal. Eventually, the robin got the idea, but it was touch-and-go for several nerve-racking days. That was the last robin I raised. Each species is different. Some seem to come already endowed with common sense; some have to acquire it. The robin wasn't so much dumb as simply blank where vigilance behavior was concerned. To be fair, its artificial upbringing with a parent who lacked the proper vocalizations to warn it was a liability until its neural pathways were established and some survival sense kicked in. *Soo,* it seemed to be thinking. *This large animal running at me. You believe it's a problem?*

Jemima was nobody's robin. Jemima was forty-one days old, and I was working inside when I heard her calling with great urgency at the front door. Her tone was sharp, alarmed, higher pitched and more nasal than usual. Sensing that something special was about to happen, I started recording video on my phone and headed for the door. Jemima was perched on a wooden stake a few feet from the door, wings drooped, tail spread. *JAY!! JAY!!* I followed her gaze to a four-foot black rat

Jemima has found a black rat snake on the front porch, and lets the world know about it. June 14.

Jemima in full snake display, with a high, rasping keey! call.

snake draped smoothly across a hanging basket just off my left elbow. Rat snakes are creatures of formidable intelligence and resourcefulness. The satin-black reptile was engaged in checking the hanging baskets for finch or wren nests it might raid. It's highly unlikely that Jemima had ever before seen a snake, but her reaction was instant, her instincts spot-on. She sounded the alarm and kept her distance, watching every move it made, flying up to the awning when it turned her way. When the snake finally descended from the hanging basket and headed into the boxwoods, Jemima flew down to the sidewalk to watch it go from a safe distance. The resulting video is a rough-cut gem. Each time I address a comment or question toward Jemima, she replies with a sharp *JAYY!* as if we're having a conversation.

As humans, we are often insensate to our own hubris where wild things are concerned. So many times, I was asked how I would teach Jemima to fly, how I'd teach her to fear hawks, snakes, and other predators. I could only shake my head, laugh, and answer, "She teaches me! She teaches me every single day! I don't do anything but let her be herself. She knows all this stuff, deep inside!" The notion of my having to point out a soaring hawk to the ever-vigilant young Jemima was especially odd. I was blind by comparison. She invariably saw them first, sounded the alarm, and led me to the sighting with a bright, upward-canted eye.

A small adult male sharp-shinned hawk had been hunting the feeder area with lightning-fast raids, snagging unwary goldfinches and a towhee nearly as big as he was. It was hard to know my precious jay was out there making her way in a scene so fraught with danger. I can only describe the process of raising a bird for release as a prolonged lesson in letting go. Releasing Jemima, I relived the feeling of handing the car keys over to Phoebe for her first solo drive. Off she goes, your world behind the wheel of a car, and you are left to stew in your worries, and the scant comfort of believing you've prepared her to deal with it all.

When a tremendous BONG sounded from the tower window one morning, and I climbed the stairs and saw the still form of that deadly little sharp-shin lying on the roof, a wave of emotions passed through me. I was truly sad, sorry to see him felled. Though very few birds hit the tower windows, I felt terrible about it. Sharp-shins are not faring well, their populations declining, and this was an adult, a local nester, a great hunter and provider. I thought about his brood, doubtless somewhere

An immature sharp-shinned hawk dispatches a cardinal beneath my studio window. Feeders attract seed- and meat-eaters alike.

deep in our woods, about the unknown collateral damage of his collision with the glass. And yet there was a tinge of relief, too, that his quick yellow feet would never again snatch a bird — no, The Bird.

That same afternoon, I heard a scuffle. My head whipped up, expecting to see the usual: two squirrels tussling over seed. Instead, I saw a large brown furry animal atop a struggling gray one. A bobcat we'd seen slipping through the yard over the past week was subduing a gray squirrel under the spruce not a hundred feet away. The struggle moved into the woods, and all went silent. Soon came the harsh barks and whines of the surviving squirrels. One walked slowly and tentatively up to the kill site, sniffing carefully around the ground and low-sweeping boughs of the spruce. The squirrel was wide-eyed, tense, alert to every sound as it took in the scene with its sensitive nose.

Death waits for wild things around every corner. I was struck afresh that, in keeping a feeding station going year-round, I attracted a concentration of birds and animals that inevitably drew predators as well. My fingerprints were all over this crime scene, from the still form of the sharp-shin beneath my plate-glass window to the tufts of squirrel hair under the

Cindy, the second bobcat to appear in my yard in August, just as rabbit and squirrel populations peaked. The previous year's August bobcat was a male I called James.

spruce. Predators and prey alike were drawn here by my seedy outlay; felled by my unyielding window. They are fed both on seed and flesh, and I've attracted them all for my viewing pleasure. It was all a web, all interconnected, and I'd tossed Jemima right out into it. She'd need every wit she had to survive here.

NINE

❧❦❧

Calamity Strikes

WHILE I WAS worrying about the obvious threat from natural predators, another force was at work, one I couldn't have anticipated. I've combed through my photos of Jemima from June 16 and find her happy and squashing Japanese beetles in her strong beak that morning. She'd just spent her second night out in the wild, forsaking the house and flying high and hard into the thick woods on our north border at dusk. Calling would not bring her back. (Yes, I called her. I think I mentioned that letting go is hard for me.) I made a minute-long video of her greeting me that morning, voicing low *burt burt* calls and grabbing my finger as I tickled her neck and belly. I was so glad to

Brought low by house finch disease, Jemima struggles for breath. June 16, 2017.

see her. Each night she successfully passed amongst the owls
and raccoons felt like a personal victory. Watching it makes
me smile, missing that close tactile bond we shared when she
was young. She nibbles my finger as if preening another bird; I
tickle her cheek; we talk. I knew, even as I played with her, that
it wouldn't always be this way, that I should treasure every such
intimate moment, and oh, I did.

At 10:15, Liam called to me. "Mom, do you know Jemima's in the house?" She'd found her way into the studio via the
window feeder. I'd left the screen out when I'd last refilled it.
I trotted into the room to see her standing in the mealworm
bin, helping herself. Perfect! She knew where to get the goods.
When she was full, I caught her and stuffed her back out the
studio window, replacing the screen behind her. A gentle thunderstorm came through around noon, and Jemima got wet. I
looked out at 1:15 and saw her sitting quietly in the evergreen a
couple of feet from the window, sleeping intermittently. I wondered at her lassitude. I hadn't seen her sleep during the day.
Just before 6 p.m., I found her near the front door, perched quietly in the thick fronds of the evergreen. *She's not right,* I thought.
I moved closer and scrutinized her. There was a swelling under

Eyes and sinuses full of fluid made for a miserable Jemima. June 16.

her right eye, like a pouch of fluid. The eye itself was half closed and watering heavily. What on earth was going on?

The next day is a haze in my mind. In the morning, I called Bob Giddings, my dear friend from Connecticut who's a retired avian veterinarian. He asked me what I had in the medicine cabinet and suggested I capture Jemima and put Polymyxin B drops in her eye twice daily. What Bob said next was the most curious thing. "I know I've seen this in birds before, the swollen eye, but I can't quite come up with what it is." Was his subconscious working to relieve him of delivering the news to me?

I was left to wonder and worry, with small and fading hope that antibiotic drops would address the problem. By nightfall, after two treatments, there was no improvement. If anything, the area around the eye was more grossly swollen. And now Jem had developed a cough and sneeze, with droplets flying from her nostrils as she shook her head. The mysterious eye malady had progressed to severe sinusitis. My heart froze and fell through my chest. It all pointed to one diagnosis, one I dreaded most: *Mycoplasma gallisepticum.*

Commonly known as house finch disease, *Mycoplasma gallisepticum* is a disease of poultry that was first reported in wild house finches in suburban Washington, DC, in 1994. Infected birds suffer from swollen, red eyes, and they weaken and may go blind as the disease progresses. It's thought that eastern house finches are all descended from a single release of "Hollywood Linnets" from a pet store on Long Island, New York, in 1939. The birds, native to the western United States, took hold and exploded throughout the East, populating every state. *Mycoplasma* followed them. Because eastern house finches are all descended from one small flock in the initial release, they have very low genetic diversity and thus little resistance to disease. *Mycoplasma* has moved like wildfire through eastern house

finches and is now ravaging western house finch populations
as well. Our feeding stations congregate birds both sick and
healthy, offering many opportunities for this highly contagious
disease to spread. Most unfortunately, as many as thirty species
of wild birds have been observed with conjunctivitis, suggestive
of but not necessarily confirmed as *Mycoplasma.* Blue jays are one
of them. Shortly after I took Jemima in, I saw a heartbreak-
ing photo of a newly fledged blue jay sitting on a lawn, its eyes
swollen shut, grounded by *Mycoplasma.* "I don't know what to do
for this little guy," read the caption. "Don't think he can see."

Though I didn't have the means to test Jemima, I had
to assume from her multiple symptoms and the swiftness with
which they arose that she'd contracted this deadly pathogen.
Though the form that has been isolated from blue jays is *Mycoplasma sturni,* it wreaks an identical havoc in its hosts as *M. gallisepticum.* I couldn't believe that this horrible disease had stricken
this bird of all birds, one I'd just raised and successfully released, who'd been doing so splendidly. I could see she felt terrible. I had to act.

In the marvelous, lightning-fast way of the human brain,

*House finches, like this blinded female (left front), can carry Mycoplasma, a
threat to all birds who use feeders and baths. These are two female American
goldfinches, a female purple finch, and a female northern cardinal.*

mine kicked into action. I recalled reading a paragraph in a book on avian rehabilitation that I'd helped to illustrate seventeen years earlier. It described an effective treatment protocol published by Erica Miller, DVM, in 1996. Tylosin tartrate (Tylan) is mixed in drinking water at 1 milligram per milliliter, or ¼ teaspoon per quart of water.

"To be effective, Tylan must be the only water source (drinking and bathing) for at least 21 days."

I read and reread the sentence. *Tylan must be the only water source for at least 21 days.* I had raised this bird to near independence. She'd gotten to the point where she was tearing things up, swinging on the chandeliers, flying up and down stairwells, and bugging Chet Baker to distraction, all the while pooping freely. I couldn't imagine having her bouncing off the windows in the house for three more weeks, as she surely would be once the medication took effect. We had to live there, too. Confining her in the fledging tent produced a mopey, dispirited, inert bundle of feathers. The tent was simply out of the question. Confining her in the half-dark garage, I might be able to save her, but I might extinguish her wild spirit, and now, at the most critical juncture, when she was finally learning to find her own food! How could I take her back into captivity now, when she'd been free and raising hell outdoors for six glorious days?

The dilemma plunged me into an emotional tailspin. I dragged myself out of it long enough to work on locating some Tylan. First things first. Both farm and feed stores in my area failed me. The second veterinarian I phoned said she had a bottle on the shelf and I was welcome to it, but there wasn't much left. My mind raced. I'd already been offering Jemima drinking water in small ramekins, along with her food, on the little feeders I'd rigged up in the trees. She drank from them several times daily, after she ate. Would she keep it up? And if so, would she drink the antibiotic? I had to give it a try.

Mycoplasma advances with stunning speed, often leading to blindness. June 16.

If I decided to treat Jemima outside, on the wing, how could I ensure that Jemima drank the medication in her ramekins? Would I have to shut down the bubbling Bird Spa? What if it rained and she drank from puddles instead? I lay awake all night, thinking circles, loops, thinking over, around, under, and through everything I needed to consider in designing a treatment protocol for Jemima. Treating her on the wing was only one of my concerns. I'd heard that even if the initial infection is controlled, birds still carried *Mycoplasma* for life.

Cutting to the chase, I started direct correspondence with Dr. Erica Miller. She hastened to credit Dr. Sallie Welte of Tri-State Bird Rescue and Research in Delaware with developing the treatment. Dr. Welte had reviewed the literature on this disease in poultry. Birds that received three weeks of Tylan were clear of infection for up to 155 days after treatment. Thirty-seven birds were cultured, and none showed infection after treatment. "We don't THINK they are carriers but results of the study couldn't determine that for certain."

Dr. Welte later followed up with this:

> *"A parasitologist colleague once told me that the reason*

turkeys/poultry never seemed to clear Mycoplasma *was because no one ever really made sure they received the full course of treatment (21 days). In any event, I hope all goes well for your beautiful jay."*

There is a tendency in perfectionists (and I am one) to want everything to be tied up with a bow. To know for sure, for example, that a treatment will be effective, for good. I decided to go with the Tylosin protocol, to treat Jemima on the wing, in the wild, and hope for the best. I'd cling to the words "effective treatment protocol." I'd get that medication into her however I could. The alternative (no treatment at all) was unacceptable. I wasn't going to sit back and watch Jemima Jay suffer and go blind.

With such a stew of information and uncertainty roiling in my head, I knew I had to get out of the house, go somewhere where I could begin to process it all. After picking up the Tylan at the veterinarian's country home, I came home via Pontius Road, a dirt trail that runs up a ridge, sparsely studded with open-grown oaks and hickories. Sunrises and sunsets there always clear my head. Sometimes I go there to exult, sometimes to weep, but always I come away cleansed.

I parked my car, got out, and leaned on its flank, looking at the fast-dimming sky, trees in the fullness of June silhouetted against it. Why? Why did this have to happen to Jemima, of all birds? I'd learned that birds can be infected by their mothers through the eggshell membrane. She might have come with *Mycoplasma* — was that what had made her so sick when I got her? Had she caught it from the house finches at our feeder? They all looked healthy, but some might be carrying it. However Jem had contracted it, she had a bad case, and it was up to me to do something about it.

I wept out there, a tangerine sunset draining into peacock blue, asking over and over, "Why Jemima? Why *my* jay?" A whip-poor-will began to sing on the far ridge. I stopped to listen to a sound I treasure and hear far too seldom now. And in that pulsing song was an answer, and it came to me as if a voice spoke into my ear.

Don't ask why this happened to Jemima. Jemima came to you because you're the only person who can help her.

"OH!" I exclaimed, my head snapping up like a startled deer's. This was a whole different spin, one with no room for self-pity. The whip-poor-will flew closer, landing on the side of Pontius Road, so close I could hear the little *tock!* in its throat as it formed the first note. My cellphone vibrated. Phoebe was calling from Maine, calling to see how her beloved Jemima was, and what I was planning to do about all this. I had to ask her to wait a moment, because a yellow-breasted chat had just flown up into the tree next to me, and launched a flight display right in front of me. Its harsh calls rang out through the gathering dark, the sun lighting its primaries brilliant gold as it lurched along, squawking harshly, dancing as if suspended from a yo-yo string.

"Phoebe! I'm on Pontius Road, and I'm getting all kinds of messages from the birds!"

"I called you to tell you about mine!" Phoebe exclaimed. Her spirits at a deep low, she'd just gone for a walk in her favorite patch of woods in Brunswick, Maine. She had looked up into the trees and asked for a sign that she was doing the right things. She was answered by a soft *Hoo!* An adult barred owl swiveled its head and stared down at her. Thinking there was a nest in the vicinity, she admired it and walked on so as not to disturb it further. The owl followed her through the woods, voicing the soft hoot as it went. Each time she looked back, the owl was there, watching her. She felt it was a benevolent presence, a guide.

Sunset on Pontius Road, one of my soul's retreats.

I held up the phone so she could hear the whip-poor-will. "The birds are telling us this is all going to be all right. It couldn't be any plainer."

We were overcome, bound together by the sorrow and hope and wonder of it all, special birds, it seemed, turning out in force to accompany us on a long journey with this jay we loved. Finally, Phoebe and I said goodbye and I turned the car around to head home. One, two, then a third woodcock started up off the side of the road and flew as a trio alongside my open window for most of the way to the corner, the last rays of sun gilding their warm russet flanks. Another woodcock rose as I came up the last hill toward home. It, too, flew alongside my car. All right. I believed the birds were telling me, and Phoebe too, that I was the right person to help Jemima. They were telling me I would be accompanied. I couldn't give in to despair. I had to follow my heart on how best to help Jemima. Right now, she was sleeping on the chandelier in the foyer. Tomorrow morning I'd start her treatment. I'd put Tylan in her water crocks, and I'd dust her food with tetracycline, too. For the next three weeks, I'd do my absolute best to treat her on the fly, in the wild. It was that or nothing.

TEN

Cementing the Bond

JEMIMA CAME IN and out of the house on June 17, 18, and 19. I wanted to keep an eye on *her* eye. She was delighted to be able to pester Chet Baker and revisit her studio and living room stomping grounds once more. She carried a foil gum wrapper around and hammered at peanuts and pecans on chair rungs, bathed in a pie plate, and preened in the sun. Treatment with Tylan and tetracycline began at dawn on the morning of June 18. Tylan made her drinking water bitter, so I added Stevia sweetener until I could taste it over the bitterness. I didn't dare add sugar, because too much sugar can be deadly to some birds. To my relief and amazement, she continued to drink the medi-

Whispering in Chet Baker's ear as he does his morning ablutions.

Jemima tanks up on medicated water, nine days into her three-week treatment.

cated water from her crocks, cocking her head and running her tongue around her mouth. The powdered tetracycline I added to her food as a stopgap measure was tasteless, and she gobbled her doctored food down as usual. With both drugs at work on her infection, I was stunned and delighted to see the eye swelling recede visibly by noon and continue to resolve through the day.

The morning of June 19, her eye was no longer swollen, though the lids were slightly narrowed. The eye watering had subsided, and she was no longer sneezing. Temperatures outside had soared to the 90s, and Jemima came to the front door screaming around 10 a.m., asking to come inside. I prepared a pie plate and she took a soaking bath with Bill, Liam, and me sitting in a circle around her on the kitchen floor. We were worried, relieved, hopeful, and thoroughly smitten with this scrap of personality and blue-gray feathers.

Wanting to make sure I could get her medicated food and water to her, I had rigged up the secret studio feeder under the shelter of the crank-out window and lured her in with mealworm pupae. If I forgot to replace the screen in that window, I'd find her in the house and up to her old tricks. Liam was delighted to see her back inside, and I found him playing with her, Jemima gently mouthing his fingers as he chuckled. Her eye appeared almost completely normal by the evening of June

19. My head was spinning at the rapidity of her apparent recovery. I knew, though, *Mycoplasma* being the persistent and deadly organism that it is, that I'd have to keep her coming in, eating and drinking from her crocks, for three more weeks. Would our bond hold that long? Would she keep returning for the medication? I could only hope.

Young birds of seventeen species that I'd raised in the past had taught me that the longer they were in the wild, the wilder they became. I hoped that if I spent a lot of time in the yard with Jem, she'd remain friendly with me. I hoped that the varied foods I offered, dusted with tetracycline, would continue to appeal to her even as she explored the vast smorgasbord of wild foods in the yard and woodland edges. I hoped she'd get enough Tylan from the water in her crocks to combat the disease. And I knew, as I watched her hopping in a flower bed hunting pillbugs, that her education in being a wild jay during this formative period was as important as her health. To confine her would be an affront to all I'd been working toward.

I was weeding the tuberose bed on June 21 when Jemima landed on a lawn chair next to me. Her throat was distended; she had something in her gular pouch. She landed on the loose

July 4: with five days of treatment left to go, Jemima tosses back some medicated chicken at the maple tree feeder.

Jemima practices caching fresh snap peas, a poor choice for interment. Perhaps realizing this, she dug them back up and ate them. June 22.

soil and disgorged a rock the size of a lima bean. She picked it back up and tossed it back in her pouch, then dug a small pit and stashed the rock in it. She pounded it several times for good measure. She reached for some grass clippings and leaves and placed them over the spot. Then she dug it up and started over. It reminded me exactly of the way Chet Baker buried food items he wasn't ready to eat but didn't want to lose. I was watching, up close, exactly how she'd plant acorns when she was all grown up. I loved seeing the instinctive behaviors kick in as she practiced caching with peanuts, snap peas, and rocks.

I moved over to the stone steps where I had a new flat of impatiens to plant. I looked around for Jemima and couldn't find her. I called. No answer. My eyes scanned the treetops around the yard. Nothing. *JAAAAY!!!* she shrieked, from perhaps eight inches over my head. I literally leapt into the air. Jemima had been sitting quietly in the Japanese maple right over me the whole time. If a bird can smirk, that bird was smirking. I laughed and sat down to start digging. Jemima fluttered down to sit on my leg and see what I turned up with the trowel. She snatched pillbugs and earthworms out of the newly turned earth as I worked. Digging in the earth always makes me happy, but having a companion choose to join me beat all.

I now found myself in the curious position of trying to reinforce and strengthen the social bonds that I'd been purposely stretching. It was for her own good, to keep the treatment course going, but I enjoyed it immensely. She helped me fill the peanut feeders in the morning, landing on the deck railing and extracting nuts even as I poured peanuts from the top. She cached them in the cracks on the deck. As of late June, Jemima was still enthralled with Chet Baker, and would descend to flutter and keen and follow him whenever he came out of the house. Weird? Certainly. But anything that kept her around and engaged with us worked for me, given the circumstances. Baker would shuffle around on the deck in the morning, snuffling for peanut bits under the feeders, and Jemima would swoop in from the woods border, hopping after him, chittering like a monkey. When he tripped over her and briefly stepped on her wing, she voiced a loud, indignant *BRAAAAAP!* She picked herself up and immediately resumed her pursuit, unfazed, as I cackled at the spectacle.

As the trowel turns, the gardener's companion watches for pillbugs and earthworms. June 21.

Female solicitation behavior, directed at a long-suffering Boston terrier. June 18.

The ridiculousness of it all was welcome comic relief to my anxiety of the past few days. She'd been eating and drinking at her medicated crocks many times each day. I had to let go, try to relax and enjoy the ride with her, and trust that this confiding behavior would persist until she was out of the woods. Three weeks is a long time in the life of a wild bird. On the evening of June 20, I was pulling clothes off the line at dusk when Jemima fluttered down and landed on the clothespin bag for a chat. *It really doesn't get any better than this,* I thought, *to have this little wild friend coming down to say hello, I'm fine! How are you?* Each time I saw her, my heart leapt and swelled with happiness so pure and simple that it could only be love.

The summer wore on, alternately stinking hot and wet. Jemima was never far from my mind as I checked the radar each day to see what was coming our way. June 23 was dark and blustery, with torrential downpours, even periodic hail. Rain sheeted off the roof and blew sideways; trees tossed and moaned, describing arcs that defied the expected elasticity of living wood. After a few hours of this, Jemima appeared in midmorning, screaming at the front door. She wanted in! I was thrilled to see her, and even happier to let her inside, given the maelstrom going on. I opened the screen door and she executed a perfect S-loop, flying into the foyer for a day of rest, relaxation, and freedom from gales and hail. She was welcome to tear up the house if it meant she wouldn't get dashed to the ground or beaned with a hailstone.

My experience with Jemima was unlike that I'd had with any other baby bird in many ways. She was a recidivist about coming back into the house. After a couple of false starts, every other bird I'd raised and released chose to stay in the wild. Jemima continued to crave all the good things the house offered: food, shelter, and companionship. And the complexity of her social interactions was fascinating. She had a slightly different relationship with each member of our family. With me, she was sometimes affectionate, but often demanding, suspicious, and sneaky. I was the authoritarian, the one who had packed her into her carrier each night and taken her to her flight tent when she misbehaved. It was I who had force-fed her when she was too ill to gape; I who'd caught her to examine her or administer medication. When she was still being hand-fed, she

As a torrential thunderstorm rages outside, Jemima listens intently to Phoebe via speakerphone. June 23.

ate better for the kids than she did for me. Phoebe maintained that that was a matter of style. I tried to give her too much formula in one feeding, sometimes holding her head to make sure she took it. "Jemima hates how you feed her!" I had to admit Phoebe was right. It was annoying to see Jemima gaping for the kids, while keeping her bill clamped shut for me, but it was lovely to be able to ask them to take over feedings when I was otherwise occupied.

With Phoebe, Jem was affectionate, almost cuddly, animated, and highly vocal. She seemed to actively request that Phoebe play music on her phone, chittering, peering, and pecking at the screen, and settling into rapturous song when her request was granted. Watching my redheaded daughter interact with the temporary blue one was one of my greatest joys.

Her relationship with Liam was gently companionable. She spent a great deal of time sitting near him as he drew and watched television, and he gave her a steady stream of small toys to play with. She liked to play with Liam's long fingers and toes. With Bill, Jemima was impish and playful. She loved the hats he wears, and as a result he was the only person whose

Bill brought out Jemima's playful side. She often waited in the driveway ash tree for his car to arrive in the evening, greeting him with joyful calls. June 11.

head she deemed a fit landing platform. When he was due home from work, Jemima would stand watch in the driveway ash's bare branches, and she'd yell when she heard his car. She'd swoop down and land on his cap, riding for a short time before bending to pound at the seams and rivets. She seemed to enjoy the goofy laughter and occasional yelps of real pain she could wring from him.

Over the weeks Jemima and I had been keeping company, I'd developed an affinity for blue, which, while it's always been part of my wardrobe, was never the dominant hue. As I spent more time with Jem, watching her fluffy gray juvenal plumage being replaced with soft stone blues, ceruleans, deep cobalts, and even some ultramarine, I wanted to dress like her, too. Glancing down, I'm not surprised to find myself wearing gray and blue as I write this, months later. One rainy June day, I'd painted my toenails a sort of periwinkle blue, the color of a jay's upper back. I'd never painted my toenails before I turned fifty-eight. Whatever. I now had a highly appreciative audience for my foppery. Jemima hopped down and began to croon to my toenails, hopping back and forth, chittering softly, bowing her head, and gently pecking them.

Like many birds I've observed, Jemima seemed to compartmentalize human body parts as separate entities from the person they belonged to, in a way that dogs and cats, for example, do not. I had a budgie named Bing who was sexually obsessed with my knuckles, and before that, dear little Edie, also a (misnamed) male budgie, behaved the same way. Bing would get extremely annoyed with me, the owner of his beloved knuckles, if I wouldn't permit him to have his budgie way with them when I was, say, drawing, cooking, or typing. A free-flighted budgie riding your knuckles while you're cooking over a wok is a bad thing. Even brilliant Charlie, the chestnut-fronted macaw, would cozy up to a sock-clad foot as if it were her mate. I couldn't blame these poor pair-bond driven psittacines for selecting bits of me that, if they didn't look right, were at least in the right ballpark for size and shape to be an avian partner. Watching Jemima croon to my toenails, though, I thought something other than a copulatory urge might be going on.

Later that same day, I heard Liam's voice, low with suppressed laughter, coming from the living room. "Mom. Mom. You gotta come here." Working on his laptop, he'd rested his right hand on the couch, palm up. When Jemima hopped near, he began to wiggle his fingers. Now, Liam has extraordinarily long, slender fingers, fingers I'd call otherworldly. And I'm not a blue jay. Jemima's crest shot up; she stretched her neck as high as it would go, inclining her half-open bill downward. She began to chitter, croon, and squeal as she hopped in circles around Liam's wiggling fingers. She tapped them with her bill and pecked them ever so gently as she made her rounds, tail half spread. Her sotto voce whisper song never ceased. Liam and I shook with silent laughter, trying not to break the spell. I've watched the video dozens of times, and I come to the same conclusion each time.

To Jemima, Liam's fingers, reaching skyward as they wiggled, might have looked like a brood of newly hatched blue jays begging for food. The sight flipped a switch in her that I dearly hoped would be turned on for real the following spring. It was a great privilege to hear the gentle song that a mother jay might sing to new hatchlings. We felt we'd been in on either a random bit of blue jay silliness or a miraculous, closely kept secret of the nest. Whichever it was, we'd made a boffo video of it. Like everything else she'd done, it had been duly recorded. Almost everything Jemima did made me wonder, chuckle, grin, or gasp, sometimes all at the same time. She was a never-ending source of fascination to us.

On June 25, Jem flew to the top of a telephone pole in our yard, surveying her property. She swooped down on two very surprised cottontails, screaming an alarm and fanning them with her wings as she broke her stoop. They leapt straight up in the air, then resumed eating clover. She flew back up to the telephone pole and chased a blue jay out toward the east end of our land. She was gone for a few hours. But she was back, eating and sipping Tylan-laced water, at her feeding station all afternoon. Toward evening, Bill grilled some steaks, and Jemima got her first taste of rib eye. She ate it with gusto.

Jemima was fifty-five days old on June 28 when she came to the studio window and, with soft *hit hit hit* calls, asked to be let inside. "No, Jemima. You need to stay outside where you belong." It was hard to deny her, but I couldn't have a nearly adult blue jay running amok in my house at (her) will. The second time she came to the window, she begged me to take the screen out, and when I said no, she began pecking the soft nylon screening. I put my fingers up to protect the screen and she redoubled her efforts, quickly whacking a small hole, using my fingers as an anvil. Uh-oh! I removed the screen rather than lose it altogether to this little blue brat, and she was in. With happy *burt burt burt* calls, she hopped into the studio and straight to Chet's bed. She whispered in the ear of the sleeping dog and he sat up, yawning. Jemima fluffed out her feathers and backed into the warm triangle under his chest. My heart melted to see the two unlikely friends reunited. It was so good to see her thriving, raising hell and playing pranks outside, but even sweeter to have her back home for a few moments. I never watched her without wondering if she'd continue to come in, and for how long. I would be on tenterhooks until she finished her medication July 9, if I could just keep her returning that long.

ELEVEN

As Seen on TV

ALL THROUGH JEMIMA'S early days, I'd been making more
or less daily Instagram posts, shared to Facebook as well, which
gave those who followed them a glimpse into what goes into
raising a baby bird. Photos of her learning to eat; short videos of her hammering away at a peanut, pestering the dog, and
whisper-singing to country music found an enthusiastic audience of thousands.

In the odd process of appearing on so many people's
screens, Jemima had caught the eye of filmmaker Ann Prum
of Coneflower Studios, a top wildlife cinematography and pro-
duction team. Ann reached out to ask me if I'd be interested

Jemima was supposed to eat the caterpillar in front of the camera. Jemima
wasn't much for scripts.

Very little intimidated Jemima Iris Jay, Media Queen. The video camera was just another intriguing perch. June 30. (Bill Thompson III)

in having Jemima appear in a PBS *Nature* special on butterflies and moths.

> *Quick question — I am in the midst of producing an hour show for PBS on Butterflies and Moths. One shot I need is of a bird, like a blue jay, eating a caterpillar to talk about how these little caterpillars fuel the natural world. I saw your baby rehabilitated blue jay and thought it would be a great candidate — Thoughts?*
>
> *I would shoot it in a little blue screened set — on your property. It looks from the Facebook photos like it's a good eater!*
>
> *Would be fun to do if timing works out!*
>
> *Ann*

I hesitated and qualified my answer. I was preparing for Jemima's release that very day — waiting for her feathers to dry from her last pie plate bath:

Dear Ann,

Woo PBS! Of course I would love to help you out. However today is release day for my sweet Jemima so I can't guarantee that she'll be around and accessible. I hope so, of course . . . but one never knows. My dream is that she'll hang around the yard until migration time. Perhaps we should touch base as soon as I see whether she's going to be here. I'm not sure we could put her in a set, honestly, and get what we need once she's released. But I must do what is best for her and she is finally ready today.

Two days passed, and I gave Ann an update:

Dear Ann,

Well, the last I wrote you Jemima Jay was about to be released. That was Sunday. Wednesday: She is hanging around like a dirty shirt and is a total hoot. Comes in and out of the house (prefers AC to 90 degrees; likes to bathe safely indoors rather than out). So, she may be a candidate to murder some caterpillars for you. Let me know what would be involved in filming her and I'll tell you whether it'd be something she'd submit to. Also, how long you think it might take to accomplish it — I'd just like to have some idea how it might fit into our days.

Ann replied:

Wow — what a gal. The filming would involve placing caterpillars near a favored perch and filming her eating them from a 15-foot distance.

Cool! I'll send you a bunch of painted lady caterpillars from Carolina Biological Supply. They will need to fatten up for a bit. Fun!

I enjoyed making videos of Jemima's caterpillar-processing behavior as she swiped and scraped their spines into submission. July 1.

Two days later, a ventilated box from Carolina Biological Supply arrived. Three plastic cups held perhaps a hundred newly hatched painted lady caterpillars. They were black and spiny and about two millimeters long. The caterpillars ate a yellowish, peanut-buttery food, also supplied, and grew meteorically. Within days, they were big enough for me to offer a couple to Jemima, to see if she'd even eat the spiny-looking things.

I was hunkered down on the kitchen floor, making a video of Jemima meeting her first painted lady. To my fascination, she grabbed the caterpillar and began swiping it back and forth on the tile, trying to wipe off its spines. When that failed, she took it to linoleum, then wood, then wicker surfaces. Finally, she masticated it and swallowed it. Success! The next caterpillar got the same, if briefer, treatment. It was hard for me to watch good caterpillars go down her throat. I consoled myself with the knowledge that these had been raised for study, and every day with Jem was a study.

It was June 21. Ann had set a date of July 6 through 7 for filming. By Monday, June 26, I was beginning to worry that Jemima might not be around, or nearly as tractable, for the event. I wrote Ann:

*My only concern is keeping her around. She is about
50 days old now and July 6 is really pushing it. She has started
flying down the driveway as of this morning, and I saw her
chasing another jay. That's all wonderful, and exactly what
she's supposed to do. I think our bond is strong enough to keep
her around for another 10 days, but I can't know that for
sure. I have done everything I can to keep her around and
will continue to. But she is wild and wild she will be. I'll keep
in touch about it and I very much look forward to a good outcome, working with Mark.*

Ann heard me. She scrambled her cameraman, Mark
Carroll, who was on another photo shoot in Boston, giving
him warning that he'd have to head for Ohio if he was to catch
Jemima in a cooperative mood. Filming was rescheduled for
Thursday and Friday, June 29 and 30.

Meanwhile, I began training Jem to come to a certain
branch for her painted lady treats. I used the same Japanese
maple that she came to for medicated food and water. It may
not have been a native tree, which would have been prefera-
ble for a *Nature* special, but it was nicely trimmed, free of twigs
and obstructions, and it was the only one I knew she'd come to
without fail. I'd begun anticipating all that could go wrong and
trying to head that off at the pass. I'd walk out carrying the caterpillar bin and place a caterpillar on a wide branch. Jemima
would swoop in, grab the caterpillar, give it a couple of thwacks,
then hop up higher in the tree to finish the job and eat her prize.
I sensed that it would be neither simple nor quick to get the sequence we needed, but rather the work of hours — or days.

To acclimate her to being closely observed as she ate,
I gave Jemima peanuts, then made videos of her from a few
inches away as she held them in her toes and hacked off edible
bits. I got some amazing, if slightly clumsy, video from it. It hit

me that this bird was juggling several things as she hammered on the nut. First, she had to perch securely, while holding the peanut between her toes. Then she had to hammer with force without hitting her toes. Catching flying bits while hammering them off, staying securely perched, *and* keeping a peanut firmly lodged is trickier than you'd think. Lightning reflexes are required, and perfection of these skills comes neither quickly nor easily. There's a lot to learn to become a jay. Jemima was unfazed by my attention, and I had high hopes that a video cam-

Processing peanuts is trickier than it looks. One's toes come in for a pounding, and many peanuts are dropped. June 20.

era with telephoto lens parked perhaps eight feet away would cause her no concern.

Mark Carroll was headed our way. He's a cinematographer who has documented natural history, underwater, and human-interest stories on expeditions around the planet. His camera work has appeared on National Geographic, Animal Planet, BBC, PBS, and the History and Discovery Channels. Mark's survived a winter with an Inupiaq Eskimo family, documented a month-long expedition to the wreck of the *Titanic*, and paddled three hundred miles down the Mississippi River.

He's shot a three-hour wildlife special for PBS. As a high point on an already illustrious career, Mark and Coneflower Studios won an Emmy in 2017 for Best Documentary Cinematography for "Super Hummingbirds," another PBS *Nature* special. But any shred of intimidation I'd been feeling vanished when Mark rolled up Thursday afternoon and began unloading his equipment. He's a lovely man, calm and exacting. He doesn't mess around, but neither does he sweat the small stuff — at least outwardly. I would be the one to take that on.

I hadn't seen Jemima since noon. She was due any minute. Mark scrambled to get his camera and tripod set up next to Jem's maple, and had just succeeded when a squall blew up with torrential rain. We retreated inside until the sun came out, creating saunalike conditions that must have recalled Borneo for Mark. Jemima never appeared. The nervous sweat in which I'd remain for the next two days broke out on my skin. I thought back to around 1 p.m. when I'd heard a ruckus with the jays outside and saw a Cooper's hawk being escorted out toward our orchard by a couple of jays. There had been nothing in its talons, but still. Restless and feeling helpless, I made round after round of her favorite spots, calling, a bin of caterpillars in my hand. The leaves rustled in the wind.

At this point I was like the father who's told to go boil water while his wife sweats through labor, just to get him out of the room. I decided to walk transects along the hawk's flight path, looking for Jemima's body, because she had never, ever been gone for five and a half hours. Yep, that was something constructive and positive that I could do, mount a systematic search for her dead body. Finally, I came back and went into the kitchen to get Mark a 5:30 beer, wishing I still drank and could somehow calm this terror, this pessimistic certainty that Today Would Be the Day Jemima Left or Died. *Fitz!* went the bottle

"It's a rental. You can go ahead and destroy it." Mark Carroll laughs as Jemima tests the durability of his equipment. (Bill Thompson III)

cap. *JAAAAY!!* screamed Jemima, sitting on a hanging basket just outside the front door. She was demanding her painted ladies and wanting them NOW.

I whooped, grabbed the caterpillar bin, and headed outside to meet the prodigal jay. Mark captured video of Jem preening, resting, playing, and whacking the daylights out of six caterpillars. She flew down and wallowed in the wet boxwood foliage, taking her first rain bath. She took a real bath in a clay saucer. She ate peas and fiddled with dead leaves, tossing and stabbing them. Jemima was back, and big as life. As night came on, I steeled myself, walked out, and hand-caught my errant darling so I could count on her presence for morning roll call. I didn't think my heart could take another extended absence, not with a world-renowned cinematographer waiting. I thought as my hand closed over her back that these were the last few days I could possibly pull off such a maneuver. She was just too smart, the wildness in her growing so quickly, to permit it much longer. She spent the night on her favorite perch, the foyer chandelier.

Mark was back by 7 on Friday morning, his last day to shoot. He set up his camera, and this time, since it was very bright out and the shadows were deep, a four-foot-tall strip of lights with a shiny reflector, beamed at the branch where Jemima came to take her caterpillars. I looked at the setup and thought, *If you wanted to scare a bird away, that would be the way to do it.* I chuckled and shook my head. Either it would work, and a per-fectly lit Jemima would swoop in and bash a caterpillar, swallow it, strop her beak on the branch, and fly off, or she'd take one look at the setup and head out for oh, say, another six hours. I was going into my second day of blue jay wrangling with my jaw set and my expectations low. I had already crossed "trains wild animals for theatrical purposes" off my imaginary résumé. This was *hard.* I carried the caterpillar bin and a struggling, indig-nant Jemima out to the maple, set a caterpillar on the floodlit branch, and prayed. Jemima hopped over, grabbed the caterpil-lar, whacked it a couple times, then leapt up into the dark can-opy to finish it. The same thing happened each time, until she was full and we had to wait a couple of hours for her to return.

From here, the situation deteriorated. Jemima began

Jemima swiped each painted lady caterpillar for a minute or more.

grabbing the caterpillar and taking off like a scalded ape for a distant hedge where she could whap it, masticate it, and (most importantly) swallow it in peace. Knowing the answer already, I asked Mark, "So . . . do you have what you need from Jemima?"

"I've got a lot of good stuff. But I have to have the swallow shot." I winced. I knew he was going to say that. The swallow shot was the one we needed. In all her brief cameos, Jemima had never allowed the camera to capture her actually consuming a caterpillar.

A normal person would have shrugged and said, "Well, I hope you get it." Being anything but normal, I tried to make it happen. I coaxed, crooned, and cajoled. I coached and wheedled. Every time Jemima came in, I focused on her with laser intensity. She was going to do it right this time! And Jemima responded by fleeing. Finally, it hit me that *I* was the reason Jemima wasn't cooperating. My energy was too intense, and all wrong. I was focusing so hard on getting Jemima to cooperate that I made her nervous. Perhaps she was picking up a predatory intent from me.

I knew what I had to do. I had to remove myself from the

A thoroughly masticated caterpillar is finally sent down the hatch.

Jemima tests the Emmy Award–winning cinematographer's mettle with a good
ear tweak. June 30. (Bill Thompson III)

situation and leave it all to Fate and Jemima. My friend Shila, a
polarity and craniosacral therapist by trade, an artist by avoca-
tion, and the best friend anyone ever had, grasped the situation
immediately when I called her in desperation. She hustled over
with some aromatic essential oils and took me inside for an energy adjustment. I surrendered and flopped down, a bundle of
frayed nerve endings. I knew for sure that I was only screwing
things up out there under the maple tree.

While I lay quietly inside, paying attention to my breathing and having my nerves soothed, Bill went out to give it a try.
He walked out with the caterpillar bin, and Jemima landed on
his head. She *never* landed on my head. Then she flew over to
visit Mark, who was standing next to his video rig. She lit on the
camera and inspected it for shiny bits. She hopped up to Mark's
shoulder and pinched his ear as he ducked his head and laughed
with delight. Then she flew over to the brightly lit Japanese
maple branch, grabbed the caterpillar Mark had placed there in
front of the lights, beat it up, and swallowed it, right there on
the spot. The entire sequence was now on video. Mark placed
another caterpillar, and Jemima repeated the performance as

if she were scripted. As if she knew what Mark needed. Which
she likely did. With her nervous stage mother and all the resulting static cleared from the air, Jemima relaxed. She responded
to Bill's carefree approach and Mark's calm, nonthreatening
presence and came through with flying colors.

When my energy session was over, I staggered outside to
get the report from Mark and Bill as to what had happened in
my enforced absence. I was feeling a little woozy from the relaxation hex Shila had placed over me. Bill showed me the photos of Jemima sitting on Mark's shoulder and tweaking his ear.
I covered my mouth with my hands and suppressed a shriek.
With an enormous grin, Mark told me of Jemima's final performance for his camera. At that, I collapsed on the ground under
the Japanese maple and wept with joy and relief. Was I invested
in seeing that this good man got the footage he needed for "Sex,
Lies and Butterflies"? Maybe a little.

If there's anything more frustrating and futile than trying
to use mind control on a wild blue jay, I haven't found it. Jemima
responded to my purposeful intent as she would to a stalking
bobcat: she headed straight away. Seeing how my mind pictures
worked in reverse helped me understand that there was much

As seen on TV. (Tim Keesee)

nonverbal communication going on between Jemima and me. She wanted nothing to do with me and my coercion tactics. As soon as I removed myself and stopped trying to visualize her cooperation for the shoot, she was more than happy to comply. I was interested to hear Mark's interpretation, so I wrote him several months later.

> *Dear Mark,*
>
> *I'm writing the chapter about our adventure, and I wondered if you could tell me anything about that second day, when I removed myself from the equation and she flew in, landed on your shoulder (!!), tugged on your ear, and then performed perfectly. I'd love to hear your take on it. Specifically, I'm wondering if you were conscious of using any visualization techniques to sort of "direct" Jemima. Did you visualize her beating up and eating the caterpillar right there by the lights? Did you clear your mind and just let happen what happened? I have this hunch that she responded to your serenity (in sharp contrast to my nervous energy), but I'm wondering if you consciously or subconsciously put any additional spin on your approach.*

Mark's reply delighted me. I'd figured that beneath his calm exterior, his mind was working overtime.

> *I always try to pre-visualize and plan specific shots and sequences in advance of any shoot. Even though I usually have to adapt once on the ground, pre-visualizing gives a solid baseline to hope and aim for. There have been many shoots where stuff really doesn't happen until the end, so I have tried to come to peace with the fact that events will either happen or not (while remembering that luck favors the prepared). Having said that, even when things aren't going according to plan, I*

*try to keep the pre-visualized images actively in mind. It helps.
In the past, I like to think I have somehow communicated my
intent with animals by operating on their time and schedule,
and many have obliged from time to time. I'm not talking in a
circus animal kind of way, but rather as a reward for being patient and getting to know the animal first. I apply all of this to
any natural history shoot. I certainly believe Jemima wanted
to take her own time to get to know me, and make sure I took
the time to respect and get to know her as much as I could in
my few days there. Her ear tug was a handshake. "Hello, nice
to meet you."*

Thus ended my single excursion into training wild animals for theatrical purposes. As always, Jemima had taken me
to school, giving me another lesson in letting what is, be. That
bird had a way of thumbing her nose at all my expectations. *Be
grateful for what you get, and take nothing for granted,* she might have
said if she spoke in words. *None of this time with me is under your control in the slightest. Watch me if you wish, and love me if you dare. I am a thing
of the trees and air.*

TWELVE

Peg and Me

IN THE COURSE of writing Jemima's story, I began to watch and hear jays with an intensity and focus I'd never before granted them. I heard and saw them everywhere I went. I could be in the middle of town, and jays would invariably scream somewhere near. As I drove, jay calls floated in the car window, and my head would snap left and right, looking for the vocalist. It was uncanny how they constantly invaded my consciousness. And I wasn't alone; everyone in my family experienced the same thing. The slightest yawp or tootle from a blue jay brought us all to instant, rapt attention, wherever we went. Never again would I fail to register the call of a blue jay. It's the

Peg, with her dangling foot, was my first blue jay love.

response of every parent in a crowded mall when a child yells "MOM!" or "DAD!" That's me, hearing a blue jay: instantly alert.

After we released Jemima in mid-June, I watched the jays in my yard, taking hundreds of photographs of individuals, with the goal of slowly and painstakingly discerning one from the other by their facial markings. In truth, I was trying to recognize individual blue jays, so I could get more insight into their lives. It's the first step in any animal behavior study. It's been a deeply absorbing, if rather esoteric, pursuit. And while I was studying the jays in my yard, I gave some thought to another blue jay I'd known before Jemima came along: Peg.

She first appeared to me in November 2013, tottering unsteadily on a branch, fresh bright blood on her cloud-colored underparts, her right leg hanging useless, broken somewhere high in the thigh. Perhaps she was the victim of a hawk attack, grabbed, clenched quickly in hard talons, and somehow freed again. I didn't know how she'd been injured, just as I didn't know her sex. I just made a guess and assigned one.

I watched her through the last months of 2013 and into 2014. Though there was a rowdy gang of seven blue jays crowd-

Peg, bathed in golden light. February 12, 2014.

ing the feeders, Peg was usually on her own. She couldn't keep up with their springy, bouncing exits stage left and right, couldn't jostle for position on the feeders, and her landings were clumsy and fluttery. She was a liability to the flock, little more than hawk bait. But little by little, the dried blood wore off her belly feathers and she became a regular at the feeders, balancing unsteadily on one foot. When she was first adjusting to her injury, Peg would often keep herself from falling by throwing out her right wing as a sort of crutch. Slowly, her left leg gained strength, and as she became accustomed to supporting herself, that maneuver was replaced by a stately and measured dignity. Peg considered every change of position and seemed to plan her takeoffs and landings before executing them. I kept expecting her to disappear, as most seriously compromised birds do, but she never did. She stayed with us until spring 2014, when the Gang of Seven, and presumably Peg, left for their more northerly breeding grounds, or stopped using the feeders. With blue jays, it's hard to know.

Over the hectic spring and summer, I forgot all about Peg. I weeded and mowed and hung clothes out on the line, sweated and ran in shorts, then switched to long pants, then added layers until I was running in wind pants, gloves, and fleece again. And on November 26, 2014, in the season's first light snow, Peg showed up again, picking corn off the ground and sunflower hearts from the deck railing, just as if she hadn't flown north, possibly bred, and flown south in fall again, all with only one leg. I was astounded to see her. I guess I'd written her off.

For not only was Peg limited in mobility, being unable to hop on the ground, but she couldn't process her food like the other jays. Having only one good foot, and that one dedicated solely to perching, she was unable to grip anything in her toes and pound it open. Sunflower seeds and even acorns, a blue jay staple, were off-limits to her. It would be bad enough to be unable to hop on the ground without giving up acorns, too! Peg couldn't eat anything that required a foothold to process, and that's a big problem for a corvid. The more I thought about her infirmity, the more amazed I was that she'd made it through an entire year.

Takeoffs and landings are more of a challenge for a one-legged jay, Peg.

I was only too happy to make life easier for Peg, in this second winter of her disability. I made sure sunflower hearts and the peanut butter/oatmeal/lard mix I call Zick Dough (see page 228) — foods that wouldn't need to be hammered open or otherwise processed — were available for her first thing in the morning, and I'd stand by to make sure she got enough before the rest of her gang swooped in to gobble everything down. Peg seemed to understand why I was lingering at the window, and she braved my presence to feed in peace. I enjoyed watching over her all through the winter of 2014–2015, until a deep snow and ice storm March 3–5, 2015, reduced her to a shivering, bedraggled, ice-caked mess. I saw what looked like a bag of blue rags sitting in a snowy tree, and was horrified to recognize Peg, her feathers weighed down with ice. Though I put out gobs of Zick Dough and sunflower hearts, I never saw Peg at the feeders during the worst weather of the winter. My heart sank. Had I lost my sweet friend? So, when she showed up fit as a fiddle on March 11, 2015, to stuff herself with food as if nothing had happened, I could hardly believe my eyes. It was like seeing a one-legged ghost. Clearly, Peg had survival skills that did not include panhandling from me.

The last photo I have of Peg is from April 27, 2015. She is standing on the deck railing, contemplating her morning handout of Zick Dough. The willow leaves are a brilliant green behind her. It's mighty late for migrating. She looks fine. Was she planning to stay for the summer? I'd never know, because I never saw Peg again. But two winters is a fine run for a bird who couldn't hop or open an acorn or a sunflower seed, who couldn't scratch her head or even preen her feathers. I felt blessed to have known her, even as I worried her through two winters.

While working on this book in the summer of 2017, I not only took hundreds of blue jay photos, but also went through my photo libraries. Searching the four-letter bird bander's code BLJA on my Mac, a whole mess of my labeled jay photos from years past popped up. One in particular stopped me dead. It is dated November 3, 2011, and it depicts a blue jay in profile,

Zick Dough was an ideal food for Peg, as it required no foothold for processing. March 11, 2015.

standing on our deck railing, about to dive into a fresh pile of crumbled Zick Dough. The bird is perfect in every detail, with creamy-smooth plumage, an unusually pale face, and a pencil-thin line behind its eye and across its breast. It is standing on two strong slate-gray legs. With my newly heightened sensitivity to blue jay facial features, I stared at its face, at the rather delicate bill and the long, fluffy white feathers over its eye. I recognized this bird. It was Peg. Peg, two years before her accident, Peg whole and healthy and beautiful. Peg had been with me all along.

Peg, perfect, the year she hatched. November 3, 2011.

It's hard to convey the mixture of awe, ruefulness, and tearful gratitude that passed through me on seeing Peg, alive and whole again, as she'd been on that November day in 2011. With that distinctive combination of facial features, ones that carried through the five years she visited our feeders, I could have been following her all along. Until she showed up with one leg dangling, giving me a marker I couldn't miss, I never singled out Peg from the rest. Now I realized that I could have been studying and learning from her for two more years. From 2017's close observation, I've picked up some insight on the identifying characteristics of blue jay plumage. My feather guru, Bob Mulvihill, ornithologist at the National Aviary, told me that Peg's unbarred primary coverts in the 2011 photo revealed that it was taken the year she hatched. (Barring appears after a bird's first full wing molt, about a year after hatching.) With this information, I was able to determine that Peg was injured at age two and a half and went on to beat the odds for at least two more years with this grave infirmity. What a bird.

Never mind those regrets at a lost opportunity for study. Insights arrive when we're ready to receive them, and if we aren't, they simply slip away. The real, lasting gift that Peg has given me, other than a great respect for a jay's tough adaptability, is knowing that the distinctive facial features of a blue jay will carry throughout its lifetime. I couldn't have received this gift if not for Jemima, who got me looking closely at jays in the first place. And I couldn't have used this gift if I'd never bothered to label and date my photos. Louis Pasteur said, "Chance favors the prepared mind." This is a dictum — no, a mantra! — that guides me as I sit at my worktable, gazing out the studio window. It may not look like I'm working, but I am. Watching birds, with serendipity in the lead, is my favorite calling. Unless I'd stopped to settle in and watch; unless I'd kept a photographic record so I could connect the dots, looking might never have progressed to watching. That precious connection with an individual bird, the one that has given me insight into all their lives, would never have been forged. To this day, I search the face of every jay that comes to my yard, hoping to find some identifying characteristic I can latch onto, not knowing whether ours will be a one-time encounter or a relationship lasting years. My camera records each one who settles long enough to allow it. I cache the images away like a jay caches nuts, figuring I might need them at some point. One could do worse than scrutinize blue jays.

THIRTEEN

Living on the Fault Line

BY EARLY AUGUST, I'd begun to relax about the possibility of a relapse of Jemima's *Mycoplasma* infection. Her last day of medication had been July 9; she'd sailed through the two-week, free-range "quarantine period" ending July 23. Her eyes were bright, her sinuses clear. She continued to enjoy her breakfast buffet at the studio window feeder, because . . . well, because I continued to justify feeding her. She'd had a troubled start to life, and *Mycoplasma* is a pernicious and persistent organism. If she ever needed more medication, this would be a good way to get it into her. As her benefactor, I could maintain our connection with food, be privy to her social interactions. And she was

Flying without primary feathers, Jemima is an airplane without propellers.

my friend. I needed her. Keeping an eye on Jem kept me going,
looking forward to waking up each morning. She was the ho-
rizon line I watched as my life bucked and whirled under me.

August rolled around, and the katydid chorus swelled and
rasped in the evenings. On the warm afternoon of August 9,
Jemima grabbed a pecan, whacked it into bits, tossed her snack
back, then flew to the bubbling Bird Spa to drink. Suddenly
overcome by the warm sun on her back, she raised her crest
and threw out her left wing in a sunbathing swoon. My Canon
snapped rapidly as I captured the moment from my perch at
the drawing board. These were good shots. As I pressed the
playback button to review them, my jaw dropped. Where Jemima's left primary wing feathers should have been, there were
only ragged stubs. Her flight feathers had broken off. How . . . ?

I uploaded the photos and studied them in growing disbelief. Jemima had been flying all over the place without the
outer primaries of her wing? How long had she been without
them? And how had this happened? Scrutinizing the photo, I

*Thinking that I'll document her sunbathing, I find instead that half Jemima's
primary wing feathers have broken off. August 9.*

Looking back to June 17, the fault bars along which Jemima's flight feathers would break are clearly visible.

found visible scars called fault bars marking what flight feathers remained. They are the result of deprivation, much like the ridges on human fingernails that are linked to malnutrition.

Jemima's wing feathers as of August were the feathers she'd first grown as a nestling. Nearly every juvenile bird has some fault bars in its feathers, but it's very rare to see them running across all the wing feathers, as they did on Jemima. I thought about what could have caused this, and my mind raced back to how sick Jemima had been when I first took her in on May 16. I'd thought she'd fallen accidentally, but now I thought differently.

Blue jays are good parents. It isn't like them to ignore a nestling that has fallen to the ground. But blue jays don't fool around where survival is concerned, and as parents, they practice the ruthless calculation of wild things. And when a chick isn't right, it isn't worth bothering with. If the healthy chicks shoulder a weak one out of the nest, well, that's just too bad for the one on the ground. Better to tend the vigorous ones. I thought back to Jemima's condition when she arrived: starved, weak, and clearly ill, her eyes closed. A bird that keeps its eyes closed isn't watching for danger. It has given up.

Studying my photos, I concluded that the day Jemima fell or was pushed from her nest, when she was eleven days old, was the day those fault bars formed. She had probably had a *Mycoplasma* infection from the start; birds can acquire it through the egg membrane. When it flared up, she stopped begging, and may have been thrown from the nest. Once on the ground, she went without food for at least ten hours, before my friend Shawna finally conceded her parents weren't going to tend her, took her in, and stuffed her full of scrambled egg. Once I got hold of her, I had to force-feed her for three days before she was strong enough to gape. Illness and starvation were a one-two punch for the little nestling, and all her wing feathers now bore the mark of that day. If they were going to break, they'd break at the fault bar. Grave damage had been done, and there was no reversing it now.

Still, hopeful optimism scurried, mouselike, around the corners of my mind. Yes, her wings were a mess, but she was managing to get around the yard well enough to find food, and it was only August. All the blue jays I'd been watching, Jem included, were in some stage of molt. Their feathers were dull and worn, being rapidly replaced. By now, Jemima had already replaced her secondary coverts and her tertials (the big, white-spangled feathers that comprise the inner edge of the wing). She would molt those ragged stubs and grow some new primaries. Right? Right . . . ? As the weeks wore on, and Jemima kept the stubby, broken feathers in her forewings, I realized that what had seemed intuitively obvious to me was anything but.

Molt is the process by which all birds replace their plumage, at least once yearly. Like our nails and hair, feathers are subject to wear and tear in the course of a bird's life. The flight feathers of a long-distance migrant like an American golden-plover may be worn down to the shafts by the demands of its epic migration. To be able to make their journey from the Arctic to South America, these birds are forced to replace their flight and body feathers twice a year: once in late summer before flying down to South America, and again in spring before flying back to the Arctic—an enormous energetic expense. Blue jays, which by contrast are year-round residents or short-distance migrants, have the luxury of molting only once a year, in late summer. This molt affects all the body and head feathers, and some of the wing feathers. *Some* would be the operative word in Jemima's case.

With her wings folded, no one would suspect that Jemima was less than perfect. October 7.

Each species of bird has a pattern of molt that is distinct to its family. A blue jay has a different sequence of replacing its body and wing feathers than does a goldfinch, for example, which is only one of the many differences between crows (corvids) and finches. Molting patterns are so characteristic to bird families that they can be used to help decide which species are related, a study called taxonomy. In the surprising and often stunning rearrangement of bird families based on DNA analysis, for instance, falcons have recently been determined to be more closely related to parrots than they are to other hawks! This has caused a lot of birdwatchers' heads to spin in a circle since it was first announced in 2015. Aside from DNA analysis, the most solid piece of evidence that they're related is that their sequence of molt follows the same unique pattern. Both parrots and falcons drop and replace feathers beginning with primary number 9 and running out the length of the wing. The evidence speaks. Falcons aren't hawks. They're death parrots!

Knowing that blue jays had a set cycle of molt unique to them, I knew that I could find out when Jemima's broken juvenal primaries would be replaced. But when would that be? Once again, I turned to the National Aviary's Bob Mulvihill. On August 23, tired of fretting and wondering about Jemima's tattered wings, I gathered my courage and wrote,

> Dear Bob,
>
> I've a question for my Molt Guru. Wondering how long a blue jay can be expected to retain its juvenal flight feathers. Thanks, I think, to some honkin' fault bars caused by her early food deprivation, Jemima has broken off the outer five primaries on her left wing (and likely the right as well). The stubs, perhaps an inch and a half long, remain. She propels herself remarkably well and has been doing so for weeks, and is even able to gain altitude, but I worry about migration, and wonder when she's going to replace those juvenal primaries. The young jays I'm watching all have perfect, intact primaries and no sign of molt. Jem has molted in some new tertials so I'm hoping that she'll drop the primary stubs before she has to migrate. Any wisdom for me?
>
> It's always something with this wonderful, spirited, amazing bird.
>
> Thank you for any information you can offer.

Bob replied:

*Oh dear! That's not good. I'm afraid she will not natu-
rally molt her primary wing feathers until a year from now.
The molt of the tertials is part of the post-juvenal molt in Blue
Jays, but only the tertials, not any flight feathers.*

*If you could catch her, it would be possible to induce
adventitious molt by yanking out a couple of those broken
primaries. Of course, it would take a few weeks for replace-
ment feathers to grow in, but they would be much higher quality and would help her survival chances greatly. You should
know, however, that it is no simple business to yank out primary feathers, especially when they are broken off like that.
They are typically very strongly rooted, and the force needed
to get them out is significant. The key would be to stabilize the
wing very well and give the feather a straight hard pull. Tail
feathers, and even secondaries, come out fairly easily, but, naturally, primaries are more firmly rooted. It might well require
that you have two people involved in the feather extraction.*

*I'm sorry that you've run into this problem. On a posi-
tive note, I don't think you have to worry that Jemima needs
to migrate. I would guess that most Blue Jays in your area (as
in ours) are year-round residents.*

Good luck!

Dear Bob,

*Ahhhhh I thought (feared) that might be the case.
What a raw, raw deal. I keep looking at the perfect intact
wings of this year's babies, and thinking, man, those birds are
all set up, why would they molt those feathers? And I was
hopeful that, having molted in beautiful new tertials, she'd also
molt her old baby primaries. But I became suspicious that the
stubs were here to stay when she hadn't molted any of them
by now.*

I also considered and discarded the thought of yanking the stubs to induce adventitious molt. I have done this with broken feathers and well do I know the force it would take to yank a primary. Those are huge quills and as you say they're strongly rooted in a delicate part of the anatomy. I could break her hand. I could also break her trust, and I fear that would be just as bad. She's already become so very wild and the thought of trapping her and then hurting her bothers me greatly. Why would she ever trust me again, being a jay, and suspicious by nature?

Do you think my theory about the fault bar and starvation could be correct, concerning the cause of this feather breakage?

Dear Julie,

I am so sorry.

Yes, you are correct about the fault bar causing the feather breakage. Developing feathers grow continuously, irrespective of a bird's nutritional or hunger status. When nutrition is adequate, the regular daily growth bars (think tree rings) are nearly imperceptible.

When a bird suffers a break in diet quantity or quality, it can appear as an obvious "fault bar." In extreme cases, the imperfection is sufficiently serious that the integrity of the feather or feathers is affected. Not surprisingly, fault bars are most often seen (i.e., are most conspicuous) in hatching year birds, because they are not in control of their food intake during the time when their first set of feathers is growing in. A protracted rainy spell, or prolonged disturbance at the nest, or anything that creates an interruption in the feeding rates of the parent birds can lead to formation of a "ring" of comparatively poor feather material during that period of time.

When a baby bird is in the nest, of course, all of its wing and tail feathers are growing in more or less concurrently. So, a spell of bad weather, for example, may lead to the forma- tion of a fault bar affecting all of the flight feathers, in a very straight-line fashion. In fact, this tendency for obvious fault bars to "line up" in young birds is one of the techniques that banders use to identify so-called "HY" (hatching year) birds in the hand.

I hope all of this answers your questions, but let me know if you have any follow-up queries.

Bob

Jemima's fall from her nest was a tough way to start her life, and it would have repercussions for a full year, until her broken primary stubs molted in August 2018. If she made it that long. For with the stubs in place, Jemima's follicular hor- mones had no reason to be activated to form a new feather; her body didn't "know" the feather was broken off and was useless for flight. If the quill was in place, the follicle would be quiet until preprogrammed seasonal hormones kicked in to cause the feather to fall out and be replaced. Pulling these broken stubs to activate the growth of new feathers was out of the question. I couldn't imagine capturing this free spirit, couldn't imagine having someone hold her down while I yanked out the broken primaries.

Knowing that Jemima's feathers were broken, and weren't going to grow back for a year, cast a whole different light on our relationship. Concern settled on my shoulders like a ghostly bird, and I watched her with new eyes. As of September, I no longer saw her fly high across the yard. Instead, she took a punctuated route through the trees to suddenly, quietly appear at her studio window feeder. Clever girl.

She could feed on the ground and helicopter up about eight feet to the nearest birch tree, but once there she would hop upward, branch by branch, until she reached the top of the tree. Once at the top, she'd carefully case the scene, crouch, and leap out into space, aiming at the nearby woods. She'd use the elevation she'd gained to help her cross the sixty-foot expanse to the north border of our yard, her half-wings whirling madly. There was labor in her flight, but there was also strength. I never watched her go without feeling my heart swell, lift, and settle just a little higher in my chest. That bird, that marvelous bird, with the cards stacked so high against her, just kept on keeping on. I felt her strength flow through me, carrying me along on those ragged wings.

Only when she flew could Jemima's disability be discerned. October 7.

Aug 18.
First hint of blue
on crest!

Aug 21.
Crest in, face
coming in

Aug. 16

Aug 23

Aug. 15
A vulture-like
ruff of old
neck feathers
persists.

Aug 27
Gray ruff
still hanging
in.

Aug 14. Pin-
feathers on
crown
push through.

pinfeather
tips

Aug 29.
Much
better!

Aug. 13.
Catastrophe!
Bald overnight.

18 Days of
Head Molt Aug 11-29
2017

Aug 11. Needing a good
head molt!

FOURTEEN

Catastrophic Molt

I'D DISCOVERED JEMIMA'S broken flight feathers on August 9. If that weren't enough, by the eleventh of August, her head began to look even more moth-eaten, her chest drab. Her bright black markings faded away. She looked like a worn taxidermist's mount left too long in the light. She was still a regular at the feeder, gobbling great mouthfuls of chicken and rice, sweet corn, and snap peas. Her soft, chimplike conversational notes made me smile, even as I fretted about her ragged plumage. Phoebe returned home to Ohio from her summer job in Maine on the twelfth, ready for a couple of weeks of rest and relaxation. Jemima came screaming in to the feeder around

Clockwise from bottom, the progress of Jemima's head molt, from rags, through baldness, to richest blue in eighteen days.

noon on August 13, and overnight, she had gone completely
bald. I stared in disbelief. *What's next with this bird? She's well nour-
ished, eating like a pig, and now she's bald??*

Jemima turns up bald overnight. August 14.

I warned Phoebe that she wouldn't recognize Jem when
she finally saw her, but she was unfazed. Because she had some
sleep to catch up on, it was a few days before Phoebe was in the
studio early enough to catch the bald Jem at the secret studio
feeder. I removed the screen, and she waited breathlessly by the
window. Jem landed in the corner evergreen. She fixed a bright
eye on Phoebe and began a litany of happy chimp sounds as
she hopped closer and closer. Phoebe answered in high-pitched
sounds, mimicking Jem. Dian Fossey, sharing conversational
grunts with gorillas, came to mind. Tears sprang to my eyes as I
watched the two conversing in a language that goes deeper than
words. "Hello, my beautiful angel!" Phoebe crooned. *Beermp
beermp hit hit hit!* answered Jemima. I hadn't dared hope that the
jay would still be coming in by the time Phoebe's summer job

ended. Watching my two girls getting reacquainted filled my heart to bursting.

Phoebe was home. Jemima was an unsightly blue-gray vulture, and Chet Baker was even dimmer of eye and looser of skin than he'd been when Phoebe left in June; he was melting away before our eyes. But Phoebe wrapped her arms around them both, pouring love into everyone around her. She walked around the yard cutting great armloads of sunflowers, zinnias, Queen Anne's lace, goldenrod, tea roses, and assorted foliage, arranging them in vases as she sat on the front stoop. I snuck peeks at her out the windows as she floated around the yard, as if I'd spotted a fairy or a unicorn in my garden, afraid the vision would go away if I made a big deal out of it. In a timeless late-summer ritual, she made cascading bouquets that greatly dignified the vinyl-clothed table in our sunny kitchen. She bathed Chet and brushed his teeth until he was sweet-smelling again. She watched cooking shows and baked sugary treats with Liam. Several times a day, she walked out to the thick hedge of Russian prune along our driveway to hold long conversations with Jemima, who was far more vocal in Phoebe's presence than she'd ever been in mine. *Beermp beermp! Skirdlp! Beep beep! Nyaaah!!* The bald jay and the flame-haired girl spoke their own language.

As an informal avian information factotum for a wide network of friends and blog readers, I'd been asked about odd-looking bald cardinals and blue jays for years. And I'd always repeated the conventional "wisdom," which held that feather mites caused this sudden loss of their head feathers. The just-so story that I and other "experts" of my ilk passed around said that, because birds couldn't reach their heads to preen, the mites congregated there and chewed the feathers away. It all sounded very reasonable and believable, but if it were true, why would this head feather loss happen only to cardinals and blue jays, and only in late summer, when the birds were undergoing

Neat cornrows of new pinfeathers have pushed the ragged old feathers out. August 16.

body molt as well? The more I thought about it, the less credence this theory held.

If mites were chewing the feathers away, they'd *look* chewed on. If mites were the issue, the head plumage wouldn't all fall out at once, since the mite-chewed feather shafts would remain in the skin, fooling the follicles into retaining the ragged feathers. And only a day after she turned up bald, I could see neat, regular lines of pinfeathers just breaking through the crown of Jem's scalp. I knew that meant that her feathers were being replaced as quickly as they'd fallen out. In fact, from the observations documented in my book *Baby Birds,* I realized that the emerging pinfeathers had pushed the dull old plumage out. Eureka! This had to be a hormonal event. I dug deeper. James Philips, associate professor of science at Babson College, who studies mites, asserted in response to a 2003 post by the Hilton Pond Center bird observatory that follicular mites have yet to be recovered from skin scrapings of bald birds.

A picture of molt processes in some cardinals and blue jays has since emerged. It appears that catastrophic head molt (an alarming name for a harmless condition) is part of the normal molting routine for some individuals of these species. To my delight, two other jays in Indigo Hill's loose summer flock turned up bald in the ensuing weeks as well. I could only conclude that catastrophic head molt is simply something that happens to some jays and cardinals. I suspect there are birds of other species who are hidden in the woods going bald as well. I've seen four photos of late-summer red-eyed vireos with bald heads, blood-red eyes bugging out in a reptilian face. It's a nightmarish vision, but it doesn't last long. As I'd discovered, what falls out must come in.

And sure enough, Jemima's crest came roaring back, in an ever-lengthening Mohawk of pinfeathers, which first burst through her scalp on August 14. On this day, Jemima's benefactor, Shawna, brought her daughter Sophia to see the bird they'd rescued back in May. Though I'd have liked her to look more presentable, Jemima put on a good show as Sophia sat quietly at the screenless studio window, Chet Baker standing by. Bald or not, Jemima was a rock star to Sophia, Shawna, and me. It was moving to see Sophia, who'd desperately wanted to keep the tiny orphan she'd found, watching Jemima. Her foundling was living sassy and free on a nature sanctuary, as a blue jay should.

Blue jays aren't the only birds showing catastrophic head molt. Red-eyed vireos hide their embarrassment in the forest canopy. (Geoff Dennis)

August 14: Sophia and Chet wait patiently at the secret studio feeder for her little foundling, all grown up.

By August 16, the pinfeathers on her head were a quarter of an inch long, and Jemima was beginning to look like a bird again. On this day, I photographed Jemima beak-to-beak with another juvenile Phoebe had named Maybelline, for the abundant black "makeup" around its eyes. They were decidedly chummy. Maybelline, who was in the process of partial head molt, was eating something, and Jemima seemed to be requesting a handout. In the ensuing weeks, Maybelline would often accompany Jemima as she came into the studio feeder. A scuffle would sometimes ensue as Jem emerged from the little feeder under the window, her gullet alluringly crammed with chicken and rice. Maybelline seemed to be trying to grab some from her or hoping to startle her into dropping the booty. Jays are boisterous and sometimes very rude, even to their friends. I never saw Jemima willingly surrender food to Maybelline; rather, she seemed annoyed by the imposition. This bit of seemingly trivial detail about food sharing would prove significant as the weeks and observations accumulated.

Jemima's crest, just dots under the skin on August 13, took on a blue hue six days later as the short pinfeathers that had emerged through her skin began to burst their sheaths. Eight days after her catastrophic head molt, Jemima's quilly new crest had a jaunty blue peak at the back, and the black markings on her lores were clearly evident. Silver-gray brow feathers were emerging, imparting a worldly look. The molt had moved down her neck, and those feathers had fallen out, with a vulturelike effect, but her head, at least, was beginning to look more like a jay's than a condor's. Only ten days out from total baldness, Jemima was instantly discernible from any other jay in the yard flock, because her crest had turned an incandescent periwinkle blue. She'd been the first of the yard flock to molt her head feathers, and thus the first to replace them; the other jays still wore their faded grayish crowns. Thirteen days after Jemima started going bald, a casual observer would have noted little different about her, other than a slight residual scruffiness about the neck. The resilience of birds, the speed with which they can replace their feathers, is a constant amazement to me. I only wished Jemima could replace her tattered wings, drop the stubs, and gain fully powered flight. Alas, it would be another year before that could happen.

Through baldness and beauty, the gorgeous juvenile Maybelline, with its black-painted face, stuck with her as a constant companion, and I had a feeling it was more than food

The dark-marked beauty Phoebe named Maybelline was keeping close company with a freshly coiffed Jemima by August 23.

that bonded them. Jemima was a boor about sharing, anyway! I kept careful notes, photographed them every time I saw them, and stored the images and behavioral observations away, as I reveled in watching Jemima establish her place among the wild jays of Indigo Hill. All thoughts that we might have "ruined" her with too much affection, human and canine companionship, had fled as our little blue arrow flew farther into the wild, the mysterious dark beauty Maybelline by her side.

FIFTEEN

—⁕—

Who's Saving Whom?

THERE'S A SCENE in *Cinderella* in which all the cartoon woodland creatures come flying, hopping, and crawling in to help
the downtrodden girl clean the kitchen. It's such a powerful
metaphor for me, whose emotional kitchen, with all the clutter and grease of self-doubt, recrimination, and grief, is continually steam-cleaned by my passion for birds. And now this
bird, Jemima: I realize as I write chapter after chapter of Jemima's story that I must present a freakish aspect, of a woman
obsessed by a bird, staring out the studio window by the hour.
I'm waiting for the bird to reappear. I'm assigning significance
to her slightest action. I'm figuring out who her friends are,

Cradled in my hands: What I'd be doing for the next year and a half of my life.

what their calls mean. I'm identifying individuals by their facial markings and wishing I knew where they go at night, or in
a hailstorm. I'm waiting, waiting, waiting for Jemima, and when
she finally appears and gives me a flash of grace, I'm the happiest person I know. I'm pouring far more of myself into a badly
compromised wild bird than any human being should. It may
appear that I have no other life. Not so, but this life of arcane
ornithological inquiry is the life that sustains me, and the one
that seems most worth sharing.

Clearly, I needed a project. May 17. (Jessica A. Marks)

It's fashionable now to refer to animals and birds as "saving" us. The rescued dog that, just by needing love and help,
rescues its new owner is perhaps the most familiar trope. But
there are stories of love and redemption from birds, too, and it
seems it's all the more wonderful to be "saved" by a bird. Birds
epitomize free will. They have the choice to leave. Birds fly
away, free. When a wild bird chooses to come back, it's all the
more disarming and meaningful.

I need to explain why Jemima is so important to me, how
receiving that photo of her, dehydrated and down, in May 2017,
was the ultimate deus ex machina for a struggling soul. It had al-

ready been a rough spring. In late March, Phoebe made the difficult decision to leave a relationship spanning more than four years: an eyeblink to me; an eternity in my young daughter's life. I was blindsided, for I loved that boy like my own son. I had one choice, and that was to support Phoebe's decision and trust it was for the best. But it didn't stop me from resisting the inevitable, from grieving the loss of someone I loved. Jemima came along in mid-May, giving Phoebe, Liam, and me the perfect diversion for hearts in turmoil. She had an agenda, and that was to grow up and learn to be a blue jay. We were more than happy to help. I think of her as a new fledgling, bravely flutter-jumping from one arm to the next, going up, up, always higher. Who couldn't be lifted on those stubby wings?

Jemima provided the perfect diversion for Phoebe and me. May 23.

But the hard things kept coming, like gravel at my windshield. That same May, after twenty-four years of marriage, Bill announced his decision to move out by fall. Half those years had been colored by anguish and indecision, during which I told myself everything was going to be all right. I poured everything I had into making the things I could control—our

August 24. A ruby-throated hummingbird zooms skyward in our little Eden.

home, our meals, our laundry, our gardens; the myriad logistical underpinnings of our lives — as efficient and perfect as I could. Somewhere, in all the busyness and the doing, in the clutter and running around of raising kids, I lost the key to his heart. It never turned up again. It's the oldest story ever told, but when it happens to you, there are no instructions, nothing that tells you how to proceed. So I dug in. I held things together for our children, running interference between Bill and our kids, staying put, buffering the hard truth for everyone. Both Bill and I were determined not to blow up our kids' world while they were still at home and needing us together. We would not let acrimony in the door.

All the while, I kept a heavy travel and speaking schedule, presenting an unruffled exterior to the world. And the travel and speaking helped. Each foray outside our enclave reminded me that I led a pretty darn wonderful life in my rural retreat, that my work had value. The world at large simply assumed Bill and I were, and always would be, together. I smiled and nodded and kept up my act, plastering over the emptiness inside with gratitude for what I still had: our children, this home, my work, and an oddly enduring bond with the father of my children. Zora Neale Hurston's words rang true for me: "There is no agony like bearing an untold story inside you." For all the anticipation of a split, and the eventual release from sorrow it promised, the separation was far harder than we thought it would be.

On August 30, our beloved Chet Baker's failing heart finally lost its steam, and my husband was beside me, driving Chet and me to town for the final, merciful act. We would have had it no other way. Only six days later, Bill took a few possessions and moved into a ramshackle farmhouse on down our road. And then it was me, Liam, and the much-needed distraction of Jemima for the autumn and winter. Bill, in friendly daily touch, helpful but physically absent, embarking on a new life with his beloved partner, Wendy. Liam, applying to colleges, toiling over application essays, contemplating leaving within a few months: time that I knew would pour like sand through my fingers. Phoebe, powering through her last months at Bowdoin College, going bravely forward into an uncertain future. And Chet Baker, my familiar for twelve and a half years, unequivocally gone, the sight, sound, and smell of him so dearly missed that I had no choice but to block my memories. It was natural

It was a long time before I could start running again. I looked for his shadow everywhere I went.

to transfer my need for animal companionship to the creature
at hand: a quirky, flame-blue will-o'-the-wisp.

Through all the turmoil she fluttered, dashing in before
my hungry eyes every few hours or days, sometimes but once
weekly, on madly whirling, sadly tattered wings. Jemima, dropping like a blue bolt onto startled mourning doves, bouncing up
and down as she yelled a joyous bell call. Jemima, looking into
the studio where she was raised. There, she watched me right
back: her foster ma, who kept good food coming for her and her
friends. A ma who was more grateful to see her with every passing day. Was it any wonder I fixated on her?

When I sighed and told Shawna to bring me that dying
baby jay, I set in motion a great wheel of work, worry, and most
of all, joy. Saving Jemima gave me a sense of purpose I hadn't
felt since Liam was born. In dropping everything to heal and
raise her, I could lay aside the burden of my grief and dismay at
being on my own at fifty-nine. If Jemima could live and pros-
per, lifted into the air and traveling on less than half of the wing
feathers she should have, then I could learn to live alone, and
live well. The first step on that journey was to write Jemima's
whole adventure down as it happened, to record it in photos

How I spent my summer: watching and photographing Jemima. July 5.
(Jessica Melfi)

and sketches and paintings. Jemima made it utterly simple for me to do the right thing: to focus on the things that bring me joy. To create a product, and in so doing, let joy expand to fill the void I could otherwise have fallen into. I'm pretty sure that everyone has some kind of void to fill. I'll always be grateful that Jemima came along just when I needed her most.

As I write and stare out the north studio windows to my left, there is a door in front of me. It's the door to the birding tower Bill and I built together, that tops the house like the cabin of a big red ship. I keep the door closed in winter, to keep the cold air from coming down the stairs and curling around my feet. And I've taped it full of pictures and placards. I smile ruefully as I read them. The first to go up:

YOU ARE WELL.

NOTHING HURTS.

YOU CAN WALK, RUN!

YOU CAN SEE.

GET OUT OF YOUR HEAD

AND DO IT!

This is for my mother, who started to go blind from macular degeneration at only sixty-six. She had to quit driving and reading, so she walked hard, three miles a day. She walked away from fear, isolation, and loneliness, and kept her body and mind strong for a couple more decades, until her balance left her, too. Ida was smart, brave, and positive, and she knew how to fix herself, just as she'd always known how to fix us kids. As a visual artist, I remind myself to be grateful for every day of eyesight and sound body and mind that I'm granted. Though there's usually some part or other that hurts a little, my body continues to amaze me in its capacity for healing and rejuvenation. The deal we've made is the same one Ida made: I keep my body moving, and it keeps working. Find yourself navel-gazing, and you're going outside!

And then there's:

Knowing what you DON'T WANT is enough to start the ADVENTURE of a LIFETIME.

Enough said. And:

What We Focus On EXPANDS.

On May 16, 2017, I chose to focus on a sick baby blue jay, and that expanded into a beautiful relationship. I could as easily have chosen to focus on loss and regret. Those would have expanded, too, to what end? I try always to keep grace and kindness in the foyer, to banish bitterness like a rat out the basement door.

And then comes:

LET GO, OR BE DRAGGED.

This was the lesson the Universe kept hurling at me. Let go, or be dragged. From my beautiful kids, who were bound to leave and make their own ways, no matter how good the food, loving the mama, or soft the bed; to my sweet Chet Baker, who had to leave too soon; to Jemima, who was always wild; to my husband, who in many ways left years ago. The wild, unruly year of 2017 was all about letting them go. All of them. And I have come out of it, and am looking back on it all now, and I never thought I'd be able to say that. Not only am I still alive, but I'm actually feeling happy again. I knew that I would be, eventually, but it's still such a nice surprise to be *level*. Diving into this book, I've stripped my life down to Thoreauvian basics. I get out of bed in the pitch-dark morning thinking, *Well, what am I going to paint or write today? Where will I run? Will there be a sunrise?*

On foot, I seek out the agrarian landscapes that soothe and save me. The Flee-man farm, Dalzell, Ohio.

And the answer to the last is: "Sometimes. Get dressed and be ready for it. Get out and savor it when it happens." After the enduring connection with my family and friends, it's the savoring, the land and the sky, the flowers and the birds and the insects and animals and clouds that keep me going.

Last comes:

DON'T SHY FROM THE DIFFICULT.

The truth will set you free.

This is my truth, this is the source of my sorrow and my

She brought me a simple happiness that could only be love. June 3.
(Bill Thompson III)

joy. I'm far past believing there's any right or wrong to human need and love. People are fated to love whom they love, and stop loving, too, for no reason that can be defined. Love is a fickle and particular thing. People come to us with needs we may not be able to meet. It's up to each of us to carve, however painfully, the life we want out of what we're handed. Wrapped up in that fluffy bundle in my hands was a new sense of purpose, a new and better story to tell than the one my everyday life was describing. That's how saving Jemima saved me.

SIXTEEN

———— ⚜ ————

The Urge for Going

AS SEPTEMBER CAME on, I began to get nervous about Zugunruhe, which in itself is a kind of nervousness. This melodic
German word describes the instinctive migratory restlessness
that overcomes our migrant songbirds as the days grow short
and nights get cooler. I know Zugunruhe well, having lived
for seventeen and a half years with a crippled orchard oriole
I called Ora Lee. A housecat had ended her life as a creature
of the air, biting her left wing at the shoulder shortly after she
fledged in 1989. At that time, I lived in a four-room cottage
in the Connecticut woods. Sharing it with an unreleasable orchard oriole didn't seem like a big deal until the night of August

*As the birches yellowed, I wondered whether Jemima would stay until they were
bare and lined in snow.*

24. We were in the midst of the August cooldown, when nights turn clear, starry, and surprisingly cold. Bink, bonk, flutter. Bink, bonk, flutter, bink! Ora Lee was flinging herself around her cage, looking for a way south. The racket continued the second night, keeping me up, though I'd moved her to the kitchen. Her tail was battered and worn by the activity, so I lined the bathtub with newspapers and released her into its confines for the third night. This had the dual benefit of sparing her feathers any contact with wire and finally allowing me an unbroken night's sleep. It was touching to witness her conviction that, if she fluttered long enough, she might end up in Guatemala. She was still at it at Thanksgiving, fluttering for part of each night and sleeping much of the day. Sharing a tiny cottage with a migratory oriole was asking more of me than I'd have guessed. Finally, she, too, began sleeping through the night, until March 22, when she presumably would have started her journey back north, had she made it to Central America. Her bird brain could neither be reasoned with nor rewired. Bink, bonk, flutter. Bink, bonk, flutter, bink! I heaved a sigh and moved her to

Clad in the deep blues of first adult plumage, Jemima faces winter. October 19.

her bathtub home each night until her hindbrain made it back to Connecticut in May.

I was thinking of Ora Lee as I watched Jemima policing the yard on her patchy wings, the summer turning swiftly into autumn. I said a prayer of thanks that Jemima was an omnivorous, all-season blue jay and not, say, an insectivorous tanager, warbler, or other species that is forced by dietary needs to migrate. For blue jays approach migration in an idiosyncratic way. In five words: some do, and some don't. Older hypotheses (Gill 1941, Hardy 1961, Kennard 1980) held that the birds who undertook migration in September were mostly first-year birds, and that most adults are sedentary except in the extreme northern portion of their breeding range (Forbush 1927, Gill 1941). However, banding studies by Stewart (1982) and Wenger (1975) found no age difference in migratory behavior. Carpenter et. al. (1990) banded migrating blue jays on the Michigan shore of Lake Superior, and aged 72 percent of 1,271 blue jays netted during spring migration as second-year; that is, birds who undertook fall migration as juveniles. However, their method of aging birds (looking for dull blue greater secondary coverts, which are retained juvenile feathers) likely overlooked many second-year birds. Some breeding jays have been shown to migrate in some years and stay on their summer range in others.

If your head is spinning, imagine mine, as I waded through the ornithological literature, looking for patterns. The whole picture looked like drunken cross-stitch. We *do* know that blue jays migrate. We just aren't sure which birds (adults, juveniles, or a mix of both) do it, and we don't know why some go and some elect to stay. Streaming flocks of thousands pass Hawk Mountain, Pennsylvania; Whitefish Point, Michigan; and dozens of other hawk-watching sites in mid-September and early October. Four hundred jays an hour have been seen flying along the Ohio River, and one thousand birds an hour have been counted passing along the Mississippi River in late September. They're moving, all right. We just can't predict which individuals of a given population may elect to migrate in any given year.

In springtime, movements of jays are less impressive, perhaps because they are less tied to the paths of rivers and coastlines than are fall movements. The exception is Ohio, where two hundred to seven hundred blue jays pass hourly along the shore of Lake Erie and estimates of five thousand to ten thousand birds per day have been made. And they pass for a long period — mid-April through mid-June. It appears that jays migrating from breeding sites from New England down to Pennsylvania and New Jersey winter in the Atlantic coastal states, as far south as Georgia. Birds breeding farther west (western Pennsylvania and New York) seem to fly south and even farther west for the winter, to Kentucky, Tennessee, and Alabama. Birds breeding along the Mississippi River Valley seem to fly straight south, while birds west of the big river fly southeast, the populations crisscrossing as they go. The latitudinal component of migration is highly unusual, given that other migrants take a stricter north-south line, but then blue jays are unusual birds. As I write, I'm hearing about blue jays invading the kingdom of black-billed magpies, in Bozeman, Montana, attesting to an extreme push to the west. Will they clash and compete with Steller's jays in the mountains? If I've learned anything about birds, it's that their ranges are fluid, dynamic, and unpredictable. When I was about sixteen, northern cardinals started appearing on Cape Cod. Everyone was flabbergasted. When I was twenty, people jumped in their cars to go see a stray Canada goose in southeast Ohio. Red-bellied woodpeckers, tufted titmice, Carolina wrens, tree swallows . . . The list of birds that are pushing into new territory goes on and on.

In trying to understand the movements of jays in my own

Ohio yard, I knew that identifying individuals would be key. I shot thousands of frames, looking for distinguishing characteristics, anything that would help my study. Peg, the one-legged survivor, taught me that individual jays could be distinguished from year to year by their facial markings. So I was thrilled when, during a three-week period of grinding cold around December 27, 2017, an unusual jay swept in for the first time. It had striking silvery white feathers on its forecrown, just above the nasal tufts. This condition, called progressive graying, affects some individual birds and many mammals, including horses, deer, me, and Chet Baker, to name a few. I called the bird Frost, and kept an eye out for it, photographing it whenever I could. After a couple of weeks, Frost was seen no more until February 5. Once again, Frost hung around for a week or so, exploiting the feeders, then disappeared. On May 19, 2018, when the yard population of jays had dwindled to one breeding pair, a new jay swept down to the birdbath and stopped to drink. It came in alone. It had two silver blazes on its forecrown. I studied the constellation of facial markings, and there was no doubt that Frost had reappeared. And then the distinctive jay vanished, only to show up at the peanut feeder on June

Frost, named for his silver forecrown, first appeared December 27.

14, 2018, unaccompanied, bearing peanuts off into the woods for a week. It was then I suspected that Frost was a male, feeding a nest-bound female. Frost and a normally marked mate raised two beautiful fledglings here in the summer of 2018, who disappeared when they gained independence. They had been the only blue jays in the area. I was on tenterhooks until Frost showed up again in October 2018, and stayed, with his characteristic fits and starts, into early spring 2019.

This is migration, blue jay style: periodic, mysterious, latitudinal, longitudinal, and idiosyncratic. Who knows where Frost came from and whether he will spend the rest of his life here? Blue jays move around all winter long and well into springtime. Pinning them down so that we may state unequivocally where they go and when is likely nothing that humans will ever achieve. But a bird like Frost, who can be confidently identified at a glance, is a gift beyond price.

By any measure, the summer of 2017 was a banner year for blue jays in my part of Ohio. I heard them everywhere I went — in town and in the country. I had a nearly continuous smile on my face whenever I was out and about, as my senses thrilled to their calls and flashing colors. The flock of five or more at my feeders all summer was unprecedented. It was a good year for Jemima to make the scene, for she had a ready-made social group to welcome her. Most importantly, she had a companion in Maybelline. Seeing the two of them together eased my fears. If Jemima chose to migrate, at least she'd be accompanied.

Maybelline finally went into heavier head and body molt in the first few days of September, but never approached the catastrophic feather drop Jemima had experienced. It seemed counterintuitive to me, from an energetic standpoint, that a bird should be in heavy molt as it's preparing to migrate. All four jays who frequented the yard looked ragged, dingy, and gray. Several were missing their white-tipped secondary coverts, and most had patchy head feathers. Jemima stood out like a periwinkle blue jewel, having molted far earlier, but she had hatched earlier, too, in the first week of May. I was still laying out a full buffet of chicken, rice, sweet corn, strawberries, peanuts, pecans, and sunflower hearts for Jemima each day beneath the studio window. I left the screen out all day for photography purposes, but she never attempted to come into the house. Not so the goldfinches, who blundered in throughout the day and had to be caught and tossed back out. Goldfinches are sweet birds of very little brain. The same ones kept getting caught and released.

By September 10, Jemima's wings were in disarray, looking ragged, and missing more secondary feathers. The nine primaries of each wing were already half gone, the outer ones having broken off first. This made sense to me, since outer primaries would take the brunt of the beating, striking branches at takeoff. I wondered whether the awareness that she was compromised would override Jem's instinct to migrate. Again and again, I told myself that Jemima knew her own powers of flight

Jemima reappears after a nine-day absence, stretching our bond. September 23.

and would be unlikely to attempt a long-distance journey. And then I'd think of Ora Lee. Bink, bonk, flutter. Bink, bonk, flutter, bink! Confined to a cage, then a tub, Ora Lee still "migrated" every night for months.

It was beginning to sink in on me how a jay is different from an oriole. Orioles are obligate migrants, since they feed on insects and fruit — warm weather staples. If they don't get the urge to fly in fall, they will die as their food supply vanishes in winter. Jays are much more fluid, able to eat everything from birds' eggs to small rodents, seeds, acorns, and grain. Beyond that, there may well be a self-awareness, and with it a common-sense override in a brainy corvid that an oriole simply lacks. By mid-September, though she was still eating the gourmet buffet, Jemima was paying far more attention to the corn and seed I spread for the wild jays, flying off with her gullet packed. She was caching it, hiding it in small holes she dug with her strong bill, all around the property. I'd see her hopping, digging with a few powerful stabs of her bill, disgorging her seedy treasure, then carefully covering the site with duff and leaves. She'd finish, then look at the spot in just the way I look at a seat before I deplane, checking for my belongings. When a friend asked if she'd be storing so much food if she were planning to leave, a slow smile spread across my face. "No . . . I . . . don't believe she would . . ." I answered. Why had it not occurred to me that she was caching food for the winter? And that, if she were planning to migrate, she might not bother? Jays, it turns out, are long-range visionaries. They're planners. There was, as usual, far more going on inside Jemima's crested head than I'd figured.

SOURCES

Carpenter, Thomas W., Arthur L. Carpenter, and Scott R. Smith. "Spring Migration of Blue Jays at Whitefish Point, Michigan, as Studied Through Banding." *Journal of Field Ornithology* 61, no. 4 (1990):419–25.

Forbush, Edward H. *Birds of Massachusetts and Other New England States* (Massachusetts Department of Agriculture, 1927).

Gill, Geoffrey. "Notes on the Migration of Blue Jays." *Bird-Banding* 12, no. 3 (1941):109–12.

Hardy, John W. "Studies in Behavior and Phylogeny of Certain New World Jays (Garrulinae)." *University of Kansas Science Bulletin* 42 (1961):13–149.

Kennard, John H. "Resident Blue Jays in Southern New Hampshire." *North American Bird Bander* 5, no. 2 (1980):54–56.

Stewart, Paul A. "Migration of Blue Jays in Eastern North America." *North American Bird Bander* 7, no. 12 (1982):107–112.

Wenger, Jerome D. *Geographical Variation and Migratory Movements in the Blue Jay* (Cyanocitta cristata). PhD Thesis, University of Arkansas, Fayetteville (1975).

SEVENTEEN

----------❧✦❧----------

Jemima in Winter

IN LATE OCTOBER, in the hope that Jemima was likely here to stay for the winter, I settled into a routine of putting cooked chicken, rice, pecans, and pine nuts in the studio feeder. When the weather turned cold, I retrofitted the feeder for winter, closing the casement window and affixing a sheet of thin Plexiglas like an awning, which kept the food nicely sheltered from rain and snow. I could crank the casement window open, refill the feeder from the comfort of the studio, and close it again.

I had a steady parade now of tufted titmice, northern cardinals, a downy woodpecker, and a Carolina wren who dipped in for peanut bits. I loved seeing these birds so close at hand,

A hungry young Cooper's hawk scatters her companions like leaves before the wind. Jemima stays put in the safety of a spruce, as reason overrides her powerful instinct to flee with the flock.

and I no longer tried to discourage them with a squirt bottle. The thought still makes me laugh — that I used to sit and squirt titmice who were "stealing Jemima's food." Over time, we reached a sensible equilibrium. Now that nesting season was over and they no longer had broods to feed, the titmice — the worst pirates — rarely touched the meat I put out for Jem, and I'd long since surrendered and no longer minded keeping them in peanuts, pecans, and pine nuts. I knew that Jemima didn't need my subsidy, but feeding her such delicacies was the only way I knew to keep her coming in so I could observe her and monitor her feather breakage. I saw that more of the compromised juvenal feathers were breaking off all the time. Every time I saw her, she seemed to have less and less wing! And she still had so very far to go until August, when molt occurs.

She didn't appear nearly as often as she had all summer. Starved as I was for a sighting, I was ecstatic to see Jem plop down on the grass next to Maybelline at 8:56 on the morning of October 29. She landed hard, not with the swoopy élan of a fully feathered jay. I had found some whole corn to offer, along with the usual mixed seed, cracked corn, and sunflower

After laddering to the top of a birch, Jemima launches on tattered wings into a clear autumn sky. October 15.

hearts, and that proved to be irresistible to the jays. Another pair showed up at the same time, and Maybelline and the new pair gagged down great gullets of whole corn — the ultimate cacheable item!

Jemima was much less thrilled with whole corn than was Maybelline, who was making repeat trips, carrying loads of corn into the woods for caching. Jem picked up a kernel, held it for a few moments, then dropped it. Nope. She retired to the studio feeder. I'd run out of chicken breast and substituted a little pile of cooked pork loin. I grinned to see her ignore the mixed nuts and fill her gullet and bill with pork, choking it back, then swallowing it. (You can't cache fresh meat, at least not for long.) She was far more enthusiastic about pork than she'd been about chicken breast. Full of pork, she flew to a birch clump and began to scale its heights with flutter-jumps, her typical behavior when she was planning a longer flight. I ran to the foyer window just in time to watch her take off. Having so few flight feathers, she naturally lost some altitude, but she managed to keep herself about twelve feet up all the way to the prune hedge on the other side of the yard. I ran outside to pace it off, as this was the longest flight I'd seen her attempt for at least two months. One hundred and fifty feet! If Jemima could make a continuous flight of that distance, she could survive the winter. All she had to do was to make it from tree to tree, make it to the feeder. Once she was in the woods, she could move like any other jay. I skipped all the way back to the house.

On October 21, I had my big lens poised as I watched Jemima and Maybelline hopping amidst the cracked corn I'd scattered under the birches. Jem had a gulletful when Maybelline hopped up to her, head held in a questioning tilt. Jemima opened her bill and briefly showed Maybelline the bounty. Maybelline bowed and seemed to beg, but Jemima slammed her beak shut and refused to surrender any corn. Having wit-

nessed a number of similar interactions between the two, I finally concluded that Maybelline was probably a male. In blue
jay society, males feed females, but not the other way around. If
theirs was a pair bond, it had formed back in mid-August, when
Jemima was three and a half months old.

By November 1, Jemima had climbed on the whole-corn
bandwagon, and she and Maybelline spent much of the day
caching golden treasure around the yard. While Maybelline
flew into the woods to cache, Jemima kept to the lawn and garden, stashing perhaps six to eight kernels at each site. I continued to marvel at her ability to fly on about half the wing feathers she ought to have. She'd be a beast among beasts when she
finally grew healthy feathers. I was thankful she had Maybelline
to keep an eye on her from a high perch.

A week went by with no sign of Jemima. A small male
sharp-shinned hawk had been frequenting the yard, keeping all
the birds on alert and spooked. It made pass after pass, trying for goldfinches and sparrows, but never connecting. The
jays quit the yard altogether, perhaps for the best. At 7:40 a.m.
on November 9, Jemima came in, flying with difficulty, loading up on corn, taking it into the woods, yelling. Here. Alive.

*Jemima's beautiful companion, Maybelline, almost certainly a male, despite the
heavy eye makeup. November 12.*

I took dozens of blurry photos, overjoyed to see my jay again. Out on the east hill, I heard her paired *Skirdlp! Skirdlp!* calls. I spotted her in a tall tulip and called back. She shifted to *BERMP BERMP,* a high-pitched rapid call. She repeated it five times. I realized that this was the same call sequence she had used as a juvenile. I wondered if this was her name. Or mine! She might as well have been yelling, "It's ME! Jemima!" or "Hey, Mom! Hey, Mom!" I felt a thrill go to my bones at realizing that we had always had these shared words, that she may have been reaching across the species gap to make contact. And with that, she launched from her high perch, steadily losing altitude, but handily covering fifty feet to the next tree. This was how she traveled through the woods — laddering up to the top of a tree, then flapping and planing down to another, laddering up, flapping/planing. It wasn't pretty, but it seemed to work.

I thought of Peg, who could fly, but with only one usable leg, couldn't preen, scratch, open seeds, or bury things. I realized that, by comparison, Jemima had it pretty good. I thought of her as making her living as a sort of avian chipmunk, with limited powers of flight added in. Not long after, Phoebe called from college in Maine. She wanted a Jemima report. While I was telling her about the secret words Jem and I exchanged, two blue jays flew down and began hopping around on the ground not ten feet from Phoebe. They were burying acorns. She spoke softly to them, and they stayed for the duration of our conversation. This girl of mine is magic; she has a bird connection. I believe it is born of having raised them, of knowing how they think, and how to move and breathe and be around them. And I can't escape the feeling that jays in particular may be responding to the pictures in our minds. The way they appear to us and make their presence known when we are deeply absorbed in thinking about jays is uncanny. It's happened to me more than might be explained by coincidence, even as I acknowledge that I am more deeply absorbed in thinking about jays than most people.

On December 9, 2017, I'd just returned from twelve days away, ten of them spent in the Ecuadorian Andes looking for birds with a group of twelve hardy travelers. It was very wet and not at all warm in the Andes, so the frigid Ohio temperatures on my return weren't much of a shock. I had an eighteen-hour journey home, getting up at 4 a.m. in Quito and finally walking in the door, loaded down with luggage and fresh groceries, at 10 p.m. the night of December 8. The trip was like a dream itself, full of fabulous birds and wonderful friends who were all grooving on it together. There were hummingbirds with rackets and trains and ribbons, hummingbirds with five-inch-long sword bills and tanagers with beryl spangles and electric blue hoods. It was just what I'd needed to blast me out of worrying about a sparsely feathered blue jay every hour of every day.

While I was in Ecuador, I dreamt of birds every single night. All the birds had an issue; all of them needed me to care for them. They kept getting into trouble, losing feathers, breaking wings, getting stuck in butter. Obligations, things I wasn't taking care of, birds who needed me — the theme each sleeping hour while I was away. I may have been having fun as a bird guide all day, but at night the dream-birds pecked and scrabbled at my psyche, reminding me not to forget my true work. Jemima was never far from my mind.

After a fitful night back in my own bed, birds still fluttering helplessly in my dreams, I jumped out of bed at 6:30 a.m., wanting only to see Jemima. I hadn't had nearly enough sleep, but before it got fully light, I filled all the feeders and washed and refilled the heated dog dish that serves as my winter birdbath. I put out all the best food: whole corn, cracked corn, sunflower hearts, black oil, peanuts in and out of the shell. And in the secret studio feeder, I filled little crocks with diced cooked chicken thigh, walnuts, pecans, and unsalted cocktail peanuts. Yep, got 'er covered.

I watched and photographed an armload of blue jays, waiting for The Blue Jay. I amused myself by making portraits, gathering data, trying to tell one from the other in the flock of seven. I felt rusty, out of practice with my beloved blue jays, but I worked and studied and puzzled and managed to figure out the identities of two of the flock, which is surprisingly hard work. I shot and examined more than five hundred frames in the process. The high point of my day was when I photographed one bird giving the high, whining, two-octave "squeaky gate" call that is thought to be made only by males. Now I knew, by comparing two years' worth of photos, that I'd given three different names to the same bird (Stump, Darko, and Little Bit), and Little Bit was a male. I was buried in blue jay esoterica, and I never wanted to emerge.

One of the high points of my trip to Ecuador was when I left the group to fetch my optics from the dining room, where I'd forgotten them the evening before. It was early morning, and I lucked into a family group of Inca jays, gleaning moths and beetles from under the patio lights. I stayed with those big parti-colored birds for a good half-hour, grinning ear to ear the

An Inca jay forages at eye level, San Isidro Lodge, Cosanga, Ecuador. I felt at peace and at home in their presence.

entire time. I shot frame after frame of them, adults sitting casually on the backs of chairs while they trained their eyes on the rafters, and a juvenile begging moths and bits of stag beetle from its hard-working parent. I felt completely happy, at home with my people. They, in their own turn, seemed completely comfortable with me, perching only an arm's length away. Jemima had opened a door for me, a way of appreciating and understanding jays that would stay with me for life.

Back in frosty Ohio only two days later, even as I eagerly watched and waited and wondered where she was, I knew she was here. I could feel it. My heart was happy and full of anticipation. Liam and Bill had been faithfully putting her chicken and peanuts, corn, and sunflower hearts out each morning. At 9:07 a.m. she finally came in. Hallelujah! She'd made it another twelve days without me around to fuss over her! The boys had reported that her meat and peanuts were completely gone every night. The pessimist in me figured that the chipmunks must have found the feeder, because Jemima had never finished her meat. Surely something else was taking her food.

But the Jemima I saw on December 9 was a different bird. She was greedy, frenetic, taking gullet- after gulletful of meat. And what was different about that was that she was carrying it away and obviously caching it in the woods. When I left in late November, it was still warm, with daytime temperatures hovering around 60 degrees. I was intrigued to see that, while she cached large amounts of corn and seed, she always swallowed and ate her chicken. If she did carry away a big gob of chicken, she'd fly to a nearby tree to process and eat it all. She knew that, when it was warm outside, she couldn't hide meat without losing it to decay. It was a different story now. I filled her meat bowl four times and was thrilled to see her visit at least ten times. She was in and around the yard from 9 until nearly

Jemima, well-fattened on chicken and rice. November 10.

2 p.m. At evening every scrap of chicken was gone, and I knew that Jemima had taken it all.

I spent the entire day at my drawing table, feverishly photographing Jemima's every move, writing behavioral notes, storing information as she stored food. She carried most of the corn out under the blue spruce that is one of her main shelters. It was brilliant, really, to bury food under its thick, sheltering boughs. She could shelter there, hidden from cruising hawks, and simply drop down for a snack! I peered at the blue sky and detected there a high milky haze, the kind of haze that makes sailors pause to consider whether it's wise to set sail. Could her frenetic activity portend snow? The forecast was clear for the next few days. Yet that same afternoon, the sky grew heavy and white, the air became still, with that sharp, coppery sub-scent. Snow began falling just after dark. Birds are extremely sensitive to air pressure, and they don't need a weatherman to tell them what's on the way.

Two male eastern towhees dressed up the yard, scratching at the corn and mixed seed I'd tossed. Later in the afternoon, as stores dwindled, I saw one towhee move under the spruce and begin his double-hop scratch. I realized that his digging was anything but random, for I wasn't the only one who'd been watching Jemima all day. Dig deep enough, the towhee discovered, and you'll strike gold, in the cracked and whole corn the big blue jaybird had been burying for weeks.

Just as I wasn't the only one watching Jemima, I wasn't alone in noticing the towhee digging up her larder. Jemima waited until the towhee left, then went out and dug up several caches from the area where he'd been scratching. I chortled as she purposefully took her golden booty over to the other side of the spruce and reburied it where the towhee might not think to scratch. Nice try, Jem. It might even work. Watching these birds impressed upon me that there are layers of complexity in their lives and their behavior that never so much as prick human consciousness. If we even notice birds kicking around under a tree, do we dream that such acts of flagrant kleptoparasitism and deception are going on? Do we grant the blue jay the wits to take action against thievery — the very thing at which they excel — to deliberately outwit the towhee?

Scientists have long wondered how birds, whose brain size is necessarily small, still seem to outpower the intellectual abilities of many mammals. A 2016 study at Charles University in Prague showed that birds — corvids, parrots, and songbirds — have more neurons packed into their brain tissue than do similarly sized or larger mammals. For instance, sulfur-crested cockatoos and bush babies (a goggle-eyed primate) each have brains weighing about ten grams, but the cockatoo has two billion neurons, twice that of the bush baby brain. In effect, the densely packed neurons in the avian brain give it greater computing power, gram for gram, than is possible in a mammalian brain.

More than that, corvids actually undergo profound

changes in their brains in autumn. The hippocampal region of the brain grows. New neurons migrate to the hippocampus, and thus enabled, the birds are able to make a detailed mental map of their fall caches. They draw upon this map all winter as they unerringly excavate their food stores. Russian nutcrackers have been observed digging down through a meter of snow at the precise angle necessary to unearth their caches. Come spring, when insects are finally available, the corvid hippocampus shrinks back. Cache maps are forgotten as jays set about finding entirely new food resources. This is how forests are planted; this is the buried acorn's fighting chance at becoming a tree: in the sweet forgetting of a jay's shrinking hippocampus in spring.

I saw neither hide nor hair of Jemima on December 10, but there was a Cooper's hawk in the area. Only one jay appeared, and it bounced from treetop to treetop in the yard, sounding the alarm. The blue jay's social system has multibell alarms with hair-trigger settings. I have no doubt that it is this alarm system that enabled Jemima to survive for so many months with such compromised flying ability. She was back by

Protected from the elements by a Plexiglas roof, the secret studio feeder provided a daily buffet. December 11.

8:30 a.m. December 11, drinking from the heated birdbath and taking meat and peanuts from her feeder. She retired to the thick blue spruce with three other jays and was resting there at 8:58 a.m. when a hawk alarm call rang out. Three blue jays burst out of the spruce, headed for the thick honeysuckle tangles in the orchard. One jay leapt to accompany them, then stopped, remained in the spruce, and watched them go. I grabbed my binoculars and trained them on the bird sitting stone-still in the spruce. It was Jemima.

I was filled with awe and respect as I watched my foster jay sitting bolt upright, deep in the sheltering spruce boughs, only her eyes moving as she scanned the area for the threat. Her strongest instinct would have been to join her companions in a headlong flight toward safety: that was revealed in the little leap she took. And yet she caught herself in time, knowing that she'd be bringing up the rear and thus far more likely to be picked off. A blue jay is a sentient being. Her base instincts have a governor; they're subject to rational override. She fights her fear and the urge to race off with her flock because she is aware of her limitations. Jemima sat for two more minutes, then launched herself like a ragged arrow, churning about two feet off the ground to the thickest honeysuckle tangle, in the direction her companions had gone. Better to hide and leave alone and unexpectedly than to bring up the rear of a noisy flock. Only eight minutes later, the Cooper's hawk landed in a vine tangle just adjacent to the spruce, looked around for any stragglers, and was off again.

Another twelve days would pass without a hint of Jemima. I held on to hope, rarely leaving my post at the studio window, watching and waiting. I was afraid to miss her, so I kept constant vigil, and I reluctantly watched myself slip into an archetype, that of a Woman Too Deeply Involved with a Bird. There has been ample precedent. I've read their books. Joanna

Burger, *The Parrot Who Owns Me;* Irene Pepperberg, *Alex & Me;*
Stacey O'Brien, *Wesley the Owl;* Helen Macdonald, *H Is for Hawk.*
Dr. Burger, an ornithologist and conservationist, couldn't use
her refrigerator because there was a broody Amazon parrot
guarding it. Dr. Pepperberg broke ground, building a unique
course of study in animal cognition, and with one gifted Afri-
can grey parrot, unlocked a new language-linked understanding of how birds think. The night he passed away, Alex's last
words to Irene as she left the lab were, "You be good, see you
tomorrow. I love you." Enough said. Stacey O'Brien, biolo-
gist, peeled the onion of a captive barn owl's mind while falling utterly under its spell — for nineteen years! And Ms. Macdonald explored what it is to mind-meld with a goshawk held
captive by training and strips of leather, but still frighteningly,
incorrigibly wild. All of these authors: highly intelligent people
who found themselves completely absorbed, lost, even, in their
identification with a bird. They told their tales of fascination,
enchantment; at times, they danced in the full grip of obsession.

At times in my life, too, I'd lived my life around a bird,
most notably the chestnut-fronted macaw, Charlie, with whom
I'd shared twenty-three fractious years. With hourly feedings
and the intense involvement surrounding soft release, I'd allowed myself to disappear into each orphaned fledgling I'd
raised. Yet I'd always been able to let them go and come back
out into the society of humans. It's what I like about wildlife
rehabilitation: ideally, the birds I raise all return to the wild, to
take care of themselves.

Now I was back again, but this was different. Never
had I had constant contact with a bird I'd raised for so many
months — May to December. Never had I had to vault so many
obstacles to a bird's health and well-being, make so many difficult choices in an effort to keep her well. With each challenge,

my commitment to Jemima deepened, as did my investment in a successful outcome. Now she was pulling away, following her clan to parts unknown. The cord was stretching thin. I was reaching after a will-o'-the-wisp, a fully wild bird with physical issues that no onlooker, human or hawk, could fail to note. In my heart, I knew mine was a dangerously deep investment. I struggled with it every waking hour. I wanted to break free, but I'd allowed my world to contract down to one heavenly blue point.

On December 23, twelve days into the vigil, with no sign of The Bird, I finally broke down and wept, was good for nothing all day, feeling in my bones that my time with Jemima was over. My family knew; Phoebe always said she could tell the moment she heard my voice how long it had been since I'd had a glimpse of Jem. Bill stopped by to check on me, hearing that catch in my voice, and put his arms around me. "She'll be back. There's a big nasty cold front coming, and she'll need food. She'll be in this afternoon." I couldn't conceive of making such a prediction, after twelve days of nothing. I chalked it up

I never knew when my last sighting might occur. A rain-dampened Jemima considers her next move. December 23.

to foolish optimism, his being willing to say anything to make me feel better.

But less than two hours later, in she came, flying even more poorly than usual, her feathers wet from rain. She hopped to her roofed feeder and looked askance at yesterday's chicken, which I'd not had the heart to replace. I quickly changed it out for fresh, and she partook, as her little flock gorged on corn and sunflower seed. We met each other's gaze; I sang and talked to her, and she was off with a crawful of chicken. The next day was Christmas Eve. At 10:39 a.m., I snapped a photo of her feeding with two other jays under the birches. She looked fit and strong, her feathers dry. She was flying better. She didn't stay long. I thought about the likelihood of her making it until August, when those broken flight feathers would finally fall out and be replaced with fresh, strong, sky-worthy ones. I knew that, if it happened, it would be a miracle worth shouting from the rooftop. Still, this Christmas Eve apparition was gift enough for me. It had to be. It was the last time I would see Jemima.

A new flock of thirteen jays swept in after Christmas, when the cold clamped down in earnest. I didn't recognize any of them. Some were pale and pearly; one's blues were so deep, the marine blue of deep water, that I gasped each time I saw it. One had a white hindneck, and one had two frosty silver slashes on its brow. New birds, strange birds: birds I would come to know with time — Marine, Puff, and Frost. I stayed busy photographing them, laughed to see them learn the ropes of the feeders and heated birdbath. They gobbled down seed and grain as if they couldn't believe their good fortune and feared such largesse would never come again. The strangers were flighty and suspicious, watching my every move closely, and I appreciated anew how accustomed Jemima's flock had become to my constant scrutiny. I got the strong sense this group had replaced Jemima's flock; that her clan had moved elsewhere. It

Christmas Eve. Jemima at far right, feasting on whole corn with her flock. When they left, she went with them. This is my last photo of The Bird.

defied intuition that the home jays would leave this abundant food source just as temperatures dipped into single digits, and I wondered if they'd been forcefully displaced from their wintering grounds by the thirteen strangers. Was it "Here come the Canadians — let's split!"? Like so many questions about jays, it's one no one can answer. The flock of seven were gone, and for better or worse, Jemima had gone with them.

SOURCE

Olkowicz, Seweryn, Martin Kocourek, Radek K. Lučan, Michal Porteš, W. Tecumseh Fitch, Suzana Herculano-Houzel, and Pavel Němec. "Birds Have Primate-like Numbers of Neurons in the Forebrain." *Proceedings of the National Academy of Sciences of the United States of America* 113, no. 26 (June 2016): 7,255–7,260.

EIGHTEEN

Other Blue Celebrities

THE AMERICAN BIRDING EXPO is a convocation of retailers, tour leaders, authors, artists — anyone who makes their living around birdwatching. It was Bill's brainchild and one of his many successes. I had a booth at the 2017 event outside Philadelphia, and I met up with old friends and heroes, too. But there was no one I was more excited to meet than Conrad, a blue jay who lives at the Audubon Center at Mill Grove. His handler, who has trained Conrad as an education bird, is the knowledgeable, kind, and effervescent assistant director and education manager Carrie Barron. Knowing I needed to make

Conrad, a captive blue jay used for public education, is held in thrall by a video of Jemima singing at the 2017 American Birding Expo, just outside Philadelphia.

a good impression, I brought a pocketful of pinyon nuts and pecans.

Conrad was illegally hand-raised as a pet by a family, turned in to Tri-State Bird Rescue and Research in Newark, Delaware, and brought to the Audubon house for permanent lodging. He is a very lucky jay to have landed there. When I met him, he'd been at the Audubon house for a year. Though he's cosmetically and physically perfect, Tri-State determined him to be unreleasable because he approaches people without fear. Not everyone would be delighted to have a blue jay land on their shoulder, and Conrad could easily get injured or killed if he surprised someone.

As thrilled as I was to meet this celebrity jay, I was still unprepared. It had been so long since I was close enough to touch a jay! My eyes blurred over as I beheld the deep cobalt perfection of his plumage. He shone like a diamond. A fringe of blue edged his bib, shining against his black chest circlet. His

Me, Carrie Barron, and Conrad at my booth at the American Birding Expo. September 30. (Bill Thompson III)

eyes were bright, dark burnt umber, his gaze deeply intelligent. Tiny leather jesses, custom made by a falconer, tethered him to Carrie's glove in the cavernous exhibit hall, and that was a good thing. He eyed the rafters, the doors, the people all around him. If he ever got up on a rafter, no one could get him back down. I offered him a pecan. He seized it, tucked it into his toes, and began to pound it into pieces. He hesitated at the pine nuts, then grabbed one, tasted it thoughtfully, and filled up his gullet with the sweet, plump seeds. I could see him deciding they were too wonderful to consume, that he must fly off to cache the treasure. And sure enough, he crouched, spread his wings, and launched, but the jesses brought him up short. In his large enclosure, he could cache to his heart's content. But Conrad had work to do here.

As Carrie moved through the crowded exhibition hall, carrying her charge, Conrad drew people to them like iron filings rush to a magnet. I've seen people walk through crowds carrying hawks and owls, but I've never seen a response like the one evoked by this jay. Was it his brilliant color? The novelty of a blue jay on a glove, tethered by tiny jesses? Or was it his magnetic corvidity? Conrad exuded star power.

Carrie brought him to my booth, where I had my laptop open. I wanted to see what would happen when Conrad saw photos and videos of Jemima. I queued up a video of Jemima as a scraggly teenager, singing exuberantly along to a country song. The beautiful jay was rapt. He became completely still. He fixed his eye on the jay on the screen and never blinked nor wavered. He listened with complete absorption to her whisper song. He became a small blue statue, wrapped in silence. People kept talking all around him, ignorant of his intense focus on the video, and one man even tried to chuck him under the chin. Conrad ignored him, lost in Jemima's song.

As I watched him, I remembered the first time I played a

blue jay whisper song for Jemima. The same rapt stillness came over her. It was clear to me that jay music reached her at her most fundamental place, the place where she found her identity. Though I can't prove it, I believe that the foundation of a jay's internal species identity is in vocalizations. Seeing other jays is vital, of course, but the auditory connection may just be the key to a bird's identifying as a jay. According to bird song scientist Donald Kroodsma, it is likely that a young jay, raised in isolation from other jays, would nevertheless produce normal-sounding jay calls. There is some learning and mimicry, as evidenced by his recordings of jays perfectly matching each other's calls, but the basis for recognizing and producing jay calls is probably innate. Jemima probably had her wiring straight by Day 11, when she came to me.

Watching Conrad, I thought about the gray area around the word "imprinted." Imprinting is never invoked as a potential issue when one is hand-raising songbirds, but it's an acknowledged problem with raptors, waterfowl, and corvids. What does it mean when it comes to blue jays? Does "imprinted" mean that Conrad thinks he is a human being and will try to mate with a human when breeding season comes? Or does it mean that he's friendly to human beings? There's a big difference between the two. Talking with Carrie, I learned that while Conrad is very friendly to humans, he doesn't seem to regard them as mate substitutes, which is what makes him such an effective ambassador for blue jays in his role as an education bird. This may be, in part, because he has the opportunity to communicate with wild jays around his outdoor enclosure. I came away feeling I'd met a blue jay with a higher calling: to educate, disarm, and charm people into discarding their prejudices about a much-maligned species. Standing inches from a live blue jay in perfect condition is a religious experience for me, and in the crowded convention hall, it was clear I wasn't alone in feeling that way.

In the spring of 2018, I met a male blue jay, also illegally raised in 2016 as a pet, then surrendered to Lake Erie Nature & Science Center. Rehabilitators there determined that Artoo was unreleasable — far too engaged with people to be safe in the wild. Artoo went on to be luxuriously housed at the Cleveland Museum of Natural History's Perkins Wildlife Center, which features vertebrates and plants native to Ohio. When I met Artoo, he was on public display, but not in a walk-in aviary. That's because he has fixated on humans as mate substitutes. He is so eager for contact with people that he ardently courts them. Sitting quietly in his enclosure, I had to wait only minutes before Artoo landed on my arm. He raised his crest and burst into stunningly beautiful sotto voce song, replete with the odd electronic beeps and whistles that inspired his *Star Wars* handle. He then leapt onto my hand to consummate his union with my knuckle. Oh, my! I was caught between laughter and

I'm not sure how to react to being Artoo's date. Cleveland Museum of Natural History, April 13, 2018. (Harvey Webster)

tears, remembering the knuckle-obsessed budgies I'd kept. My hand was the hen of their dreams. There was something hilarious, yet deeply sad about the whole performance.

Would his obsessive courting behavior, undoubtedly born of long isolation and sexual frustration, persist if Artoo were given the opportunity to interact with other birds? Things are looking up for him. Harvey Webster, chief wildlife officer and museum ambassador at CMNH, transitioned Artoo to a large walk-in aviary with another male jay and an assortment of larger birds in November 2018. The staff is eagerly watching to see what changes in Artoo's behavior may result from more space and other birds with whom he can interact. Artoo is a treasured member of the Perkins Wildlife Center family.

"Everyone who sees him up close says, 'Oh my God! Look how beautiful he is!'" Harvey says. "To have him bobbing and highly interactive, doing his *beedle beedle* call, is just amazing . . . At Perkins, we're trying to create that spearhead to exploration and discovery with Ohio creatures and plants. The first step to getting people to give a damn is awareness. Even the common things, like a blue jay—to see it up close, to see the amazing

Harvey Webster, CMNH's director of wildlife and ambassador, with his beloved charge Artoo.

colors, hear its vocal acrobatics. You see it in a new light. That
leads . . . to the possibility that a door opens and the light comes
in. And perhaps to an awareness of the need to conserve them."

Artoo, like Conrad, had an unfortunate start in life that
has evolved into a public ambassadorship. Not all blue jays
taken from the wild are nearly so lucky. Artoo showed me what
an imprinted blue jay looks like. It is possible to transmute the
social identity of a blue jay by keeping it isolated from its kind
and confining it past sexual maturity without contact with its
own kind. It's possible, but you have to work at it for a long
time, as did the family who raised him, thinking it would be
fun, then had to surrender the bird. There are many reasons it's
illegal to keep native birds as pets. Such exploitation still leads
to the demise and extinction of many species worldwide. They
were never meant to be confined and taken away from their
own kind. And (take it from one who was tearing her hair by
the time Jemima was ready for release) jays are messy, horrible,
destructive house pets. Caging a jay as if it were a parakeet? Un-
thinkable. But people still try it, and quickly realize they are in
over their heads trying to confine a brilliant, highly social corvid. Word gets out, and most such "pets" will be confiscated,
and their keepers fined.

Jays that are illegally kept past the point when they should
have been released will show the effects for the rest of their
lives. Yet hand-raising does not by any means spell doom for
a jay's future social life. Learning about another well-known
blue jay helped me refine my thinking about the whole issue.
Gracie first came to public attention in a video clip aired on
the popular video aggregator, the Dodo, in August 2017, but his
story had been unfolding for two years. Gracie was found on
the ground when he was very young and taken in for care by the
Theissen family in their Florida home in the spring of 2015. He
was a spiky porcupine; his feathers had yet to erupt. His eyes

were not yet open. He looked to be around Day 7 (Jemima was an estimated eleven days old when she came to me). The popular assumption about blue jays is that they are much more likely to imprint on human caretakers if their eyes are still sealed when taken in. By this measure, Gracie qualified as an imprinting risk. But Dina and Ken Theissen kept Gracie on a screened porch, where he could hear and see neighborhood jays. Their intent was always to raise him for return to the wild. Gracie was one of the lucky ones.

The Theissens made their first attempt to release Gracie outside at about thirty days of age, but he came right back into the house. Daily attempts finally took by Day 35, and Gracie decided to stay outside, though he was able to come and go from the house through a hole in the porch screen. Striking a balance in their relationship based on the bird's free will, the Theissens have watched Gracie pair with a wild female and raise, by the fall of 2018, six broods of young with her! Despite having lived in the wild for three years, Gracie has chosen not to cut the ties with his human family. He freely perches on their hands; he navigates every corner of their house and was still coming in for visits as of March 2019. A nicely stocked pantry and clean bathing saucers on the porch provide continuing incentive. His mate and offspring occasionally follow Gracie onto the porch for treats, though they have trouble navigating the porch screen hole the acclimated jay uses with ease. Gracie leads a full, wild life, dipping in and out to visit his foster human family while raising brood after brood with a wild mate.

Gracie's example, and Jemima's as well, casts into serious doubt the dictum that a hand-raised blue jay will be ruined for life, that it will identify as human and be unable to make meaningful social contact with its own species. Gracie, all by himself, puts the lie to the popular directive to isolate young jays, to keep them together in darkened rooms or covered cages lest they imprint on their human caretakers. He and Jemima were both raised alone in a human household, yet neither showed much hesitation in reentering jay society. The Florida family's experience is all the more remarkable because Gracie never saw another jay before he fell out of his nest.

But Gracie had heard his parents calling, and he doubtless was able to hear and see his family from the screened porch as he grew. He and Jemima had their identities set, probably innately, with the reinforcement of seeing and hearing wild jays throughout their hand-rearing period. As for strictly limiting human contact to "prevent imprinting," there is no fooling a blue jay. You might dart in, feed it quickly, and cover its cage again, but no amount of precaution will trick it into thinking it never saw you or received food from you. The bond that results from your caring for it can be stretchy and long-lived, as in Gracie's case, or it can break at the moment of release. The key to a successful release is timing, to release the bird just as soon as it is taking all its food from a dish and no longer needs hand-feeding. That would be around forty days of age. Turning it out into the wild, where it can use innate call recognition to find its own kind, prepares it for finding an appropriate mate by the time it is sexually mature the next spring.

Being affectionate, within reason, toward a young bird you're raising won't — can't — forever alter its species identity. I don't stroke or pet my young birds, but neither do I keep them in solitary confinement, avert my eyes, or remain silent around them. I frankly find that kind of self-imposed restraint, often mandated by larger wildlife rehab centers in an attempt to avoid the kind of emotional attachment referred to as "bunny hugging," ridiculous. I talk to the birds I raise, interact with them, give them names and toys; I allow them to ride on my hand or shoulder; I pick them up when I need to and handle them as much as I have to, to keep them well-fed, clean, and comfortable. I often jokingly refer to the wild birds I raise as "my clients," and that's what they are: temporary residents, destined for release. They live in my kitchen and living room, fed on the hour, until they're ready for a flight tent. Jemima spent most of her nestling and post-fledging period perched on the backs of our kitchen chairs near a large window. She could see and hear the local jays coming in for seed and peanuts on the banister just outside, and she gave them her undivided attention whenever they bounced onto the railing.

It was clear that Jemima knew she was a blue jay, as did Gracie, despite being very young when orphaned. All my endearments, my words, even my name for her were no more than background noise to Jemima. What mattered to her were blue jay calls, and those were hardwired in the densely packed neurons of her brain. There was no changing that fact with any amount of caring intervention.

It's best to hand-raise jays with others of their kind. If that isn't possible, keeping them within earshot and sight of wild jays is a good substitute. If other jays aren't around, it's a simple matter in the Information Age to play jay calls for them, to show video. This should bolster their nestling memories and their innate recognition of other jays, and help keep their self-identity on track. Unlike dogs, birds readily watch and respond to two-dimensional images, especially video. The best blue jay video and behavioral observation available comes from the west coast of Newfoundland, created by a researcher who's accessible on YouTube and all major social media platforms as LesleytheBirdNerd. Since 2011, she's been using food enticements to build a relationship with wild blue jays that must be seen to be believed. Lesley has her flock members named and follows individuals and their familial relationships for years on end. It takes a dedicated individual, willing to look closely, take thousands of photos, and put boots on the ground, to crack some of

Josie, Caledonia, and Lou, three orphaned jays I was privileged to care for in the summer of 2018. August 14, 2018.

the blue jays' secrets, and Lesley's the one who's doing it. Each little interaction might help answer a question. And there are so many questions.

In late summer of 2018, I was asked by the Ohio Wildlife Center to release three hand-raised orphaned blue jays on our sanctuary. Phoebe, Liam, and I set up a tent in the open garage for the trio we named Lou, Josie, and Caledonia, expecting to hold them for a few days, just until they got the lay of the land. But on the morning slated for release, Lou was clearly ill, and over the next few days, he developed a full-blown case of avian pox. Lou went back to the hospital, and I was left with two apparently healthy jays who had been exposed to this terrible disease. I consulted with Dr. Erica Miller and decided to quarantine the two healthy jays in the flight tent past the incubation period of pox before releasing them. All told, I had to hold them for three weeks. They were self-feeding and more than ready for release when I got them, so this took some doing.

With each other in the flight tent for company, Josie and Cal came through quarantine with flying colors, delighting us with their distinct personalities and nonstop shenanigans. They were acclimated to humans but not tame or docile;

OWC staff and volunteers had done a good job. On the rare occasions they landed on my arm, they were far more likely to pound a hole in me than cuddle up to me! We kept an enriched environment in the big tent, full of live insects to hunt, nuts to open, and shiny toys to hide. Phoebe, Liam, and I spent hours watching them interact, sitting quietly in camp chairs inside the tent while wearing "blue jay bling" — costume jewelry that they'd come to inspect and steal. Their finest hour came when I found an overturned planter in my flower bed with perhaps five dozen camel crickets clinging inside it. Pure gold! Gingerly, I tiptoed it into the tent and turned it on its side. The pot was like a magic cricket gumball machine, and the big, juicy insects sporadically bounced out and hid in every corner. The jays had a ball ferreting out nearly every one, starting their daily hunt before light, when the crickets were active. When I finally cleaned out the tent, I found only two thoroughly shell-shocked crickets. The orphans' insect-foraging skills were razor-sharp.

Every day, when I opened the garage doors so the orphans could enjoy the view from their flight tent, the wild jays who lived on our sanctuary would come to visit, calling back and

Caledonia steals a Lego toy from Josie in their temporary flight tent home.

forth. One even flew into the open garage and hovered at the side of the flight tent where Phoebe was sitting quietly with our clients. I figured something was going on between the birds, but I never could have predicted what would happen on the orphans' release. On the morning we finally unzipped the tent, Josie and Caledonia flew to the top of a nearby ash and screamed lustily. It seemed a very odd way to go into the wide-open world; Jemima had been perfectly silent and furtive for the first week after release. Their madness had a method.

Within seconds, four blue jays arrived, calling excitedly with friendly *hit hit hit* notes. They hopped and fluttered between the orphans. And within a few minutes, Josie and Cal were just voices in the north border, spirited away by their new friends. I saw and heard the two a handful of times in the weeks that ensued, but they never came back for food or companionship again. They never needed to. I have little doubt that being raised with other jays, and having the opportunity to be in the presence of wild jays, contributed to their instant inclusion into the flock. After all, they'd already met. Perhaps they'd all collaborated on the escape plan while the orphans were still in the hoosegow. Anything's possible with the corvid brain. Still, I was dizzy at the speed with which the two quit the premises and never looked back — what a contrast with Jemima's arc! I had heard anecdotes of a woman in Texas who raised and released orphaned blue jays, claiming that wild jays always swooped in and adopted them immediately upon release. It sounded like someone else's fairy tale until it happened in my own yard. And it is unique in my experience of raising songbirds for release.

It is human hubris, a vast overestimation of our own importance to the orphaned songbirds we raise, I believe, that causes us to fear we will "ruin" corvids through imprinting by hand-raising. It's the same self-importance that makes us think we must teach them basic survival skills. It's clear to me after five decades of raising songbirds that they come to us already knowing everything they need to survive in the wild. They just need the care and support to develop those instinctual skills in safety. Gracie's and Jemima's stories strongly challenge the notion that blue jays, raised singly in captivity, risk becoming hopelessly imprinted and unreleasable. Their experiences show that affection and social interaction do not spoil a young jay; rather the socialization enriches and strengthens it. The trick is letting the bird go between Days 35 and 40, or as soon as it is self-feeding and ready for release. Most humans are bad at judging when a bird is ready; hence the age recommendation. The colorful, varied, rich world outside holds a lesson at every turn, and a young bird swiftly comes to prefer the freedom of flying to the top of a tree, choosing its own roosting spot, and finding others of its kind to the confines of a house and human care. Given half a chance to rejoin the society to which it instinctively cleaves — the one whose words and music speak to it — a jay will grab it, fly with it, and never look back.

NINETEEN

───────── ✦ ─────────

Lessons from a Jay

ON THE EVENING of April 4, 2018, I was crouching tautly on a couch (sitting would be a poor descriptor), waiting for Jemima to appear. This time, though, my eyes were directed not out the studio window, but on the TV screen in my living room. PBS *Nature*'s "Sex, Lies and Butterflies" was airing tonight, and Jemima was to make her international television debut in the role of Caterpillar Predator. A painted lady caterpillar crawled along the smooth branch of a Japanese maple. Ominous tones, recalling the attack scenes in *Jaws,* rasped as a beautiful blue jay hopped springily into view. Snap! Jemima snatched the caterpillar, swabbed it on the branch, masticated and swallowed

I'd like to believe that, wherever Jemima has gone since I last saw her on Christmas Eve 2017, she is making her way, Maybelline by her side.

it, all in dreamy slow motion. And again! Another caterpillar (hand-raised by me) met its fate. A kettle drum boomed with each attack. Paul Giamatti, an actor I greatly admire, lent his voice-over to the show, describing Jemima as "a young blue jay, no longer being fed by its parents." I chuckled. Technically, that was true. Jemima had last been fed by her birth parents sometime on May 16. The sequence was videotaped on June 30. But oh, the time in between . . . How precious it had been to her foster family. And now here she was on millions of television screens, masquerading as a wild blue jay. Well, by the end of June, she *was* wild.

In conceiving this book, I was swept away by the hope and the great, foolish notion that I would get to see Jemima through her first winter, even her first year. That she'd somehow struggle through it and come out on the other side in spring, when the living got easier. That she and Maybelline would mate and raise a brood and maybe even bring them to the secret studio feeder to gorge on my home cooking. That I'd be here on the July day when she dropped the stub of her first broken wing feather, and I'd get to see her ply the air in September 2018

Jemima's star turn on PBS Nature's "Sex, Lies and Butterflies." (Tim Keesee)

on a pair of beautiful, fully feathered wings. That she would emerge from her star-crossed life unbroken. I dreamt. Oh, how I dreamt. But I knew that, no matter how it might end, Jemima's story was worth telling.

I haven't seen The Bird since December 24, 2017. Letting her go has been incredibly difficult. I scrutinize and photograph every jay that comes into the yard. I have had to force myself to stop wondering what became of her, make myself look back on the experience of raising her, and realize that it is — it has to be — enough. That as much as I might want to tie her story up with a bow and a nest full of baby jays, I won't be able to. I ask myself what Jemima taught me, what sweet, whole grains of knowledge I can winnow out of the great double handful of work and worry and responsibility that raising her entailed.

First, and probably most important, Jemima taught me that there is a wisdom, even in a young, orphaned blue jay, that should humble anyone who pays attention. Always look to the bird for guidance. Stand back and let the bird be herself. If she becomes depressed and anorexic when left alone, bring her back in the house! Play music for her. Ask her to leap from arm to arm. Laugh with her. Play with her. She's telling you what she needs. Provide it. Do not be afraid to interact, to engage her.

Second, the notion that by hand-raising a jay you could "ruin" her and render her unreleasable because she'll imprint on humans is a conceit of humans and a reflection of our disconnect with nature. In my view, this assumption does blue jays disrespect. No matter how much we might imagine that the world revolves around us, a wild jay, however it is raised, is pre-adapted and programmed to be wild. She will always be alert and listening for the calls and sounds, the words and music that make sense to her. Give her the society of jays, and she will rush to join it. You, as a human, barely rank by comparison.

Third, as hard as it was to grapple with, I learned volumes

It would be impossible for me not to engage a sprite like Jemima. June 4.

from Jemima's illness. The misfortune of having contracted *My-coplasma,* perhaps in the egg, is likely what made her too weak to compete with her siblings and tossed her from the nest. If I've learned anything from Jemima's experience, and that of Stuart, her ill-fated companion, it's that a young bird found on the ground may be there for good reason. The cards may well be stacked against it, and anyone raising such a foundling had better buckle in for the ride. How could I have known that Jemima's illness as a nestling would lead to her flight feathers breaking off when she was a robust juvenile and apparently cured of her disease? Another lesson learned. The greater gift: her misfortune made Jemima a valuable test subject for the three-week Tylosin antibiotic protocol developed by Sallie Welte and Erica Miller. After her treatment ended July 9, Jemima was symptom-free for at least another five and a half months, lending another hard-to-get data point and further credence to this protocol. That I could keep our bond strong for the three weeks it took to administer the drug to a free-living bird was something for which I remain grateful. That I could thereby effect an apparent cure, following her until Christmas, and reporting back to the people who devised it, was a gift beyond measure.

Fourth, I've realized that individual jays can be distinguished from year to year by subtle differences in their markings. That was a gift from Peg, the one-legged survivor, the first blue jay I fell for. The gift keeps giving. Each jay I see here joins a rogues' gallery of photographs, each one dated. And why not? Over time, I may be able to piece together the stories of more individual jays, with silver-browed Frost at the helm. Cracking a portal on blue jay society has been a deeply humbling experience. It's like putting together a jigsaw puzzle, piece by tiny piece, when you're handed one or two random pieces, once every couple of months. The first credo of intelligent tinkering is to keep all the pieces.

Fifth, it is their very intelligence that keeps jays a mystery to us. I realize that, short of netting and color-banding each bird in the yard, I will never know for certain which jays "belong" here and which are birds of passage. Curtis Adkisson, who for years studied nut dispersal by blue jays at Archbold Biological Station in Florida, noted that if he set nets and caught several jays, he would never be able to capture jays at that location again. Nor was he ever able to recapture any marked birds. Nets had to be moved to a completely different location if he

Phoebe "inflates" Jemima by breathing on the back of her neck. (Phoebe Linnea Thompson)

Slight differences in the amount and extent of their black facial markings give this mated pair of blue jays distinctively different expressions. Not all are this easy to differentiate.

was to have any hope of capturing and marking more blue jays. Once caught, twice shy. There's a reason the ornithological literature on blue jays is slim. They're too smart to allow themselves to be trapped, color marked, recaptured, studied. It figures that my favorite bird would be too smart to study by any conventional means. Their intelligence is what draws me and keeps me in the blue jays' thrall. I'll stay behind my telephoto lens, making my noninvasive but thoroughly enjoyable observations, as long as I'm able.

Sixth, Jemima showed me how to let go and be grateful for what I was given. When you get a puppy, you can pretty much count on a decade of companionship, barring accident or illness. When you raise a wild bird, all bets are off. When I took Jemima on, I rolled my heart into a crapshoot. Fate made all the calls. Fate always does. Whether in life, marriage, or bird rehabilitation, things rarely work out the way you envision, hope, dream, or plan for. Jemima showed me how hard I hang on to the ones I love, even as they are trying to leave. Setting one's heart on maintaining a connection with a wild bird, who is compelled to follow her own flock, is an object lesson in letting go. Let go, or be dragged. It could be tattooed on my arm, if I were the kind to go for tattoos. There's nothing to stop me from writing it in laundry marker. Maybe it'd help.

Seventh, Jemima took me to school on nonverbal communication with animals. I firmly believe that they can see what you're envisioning. Exchanging mind pictures with animals is a real and powerful way to reach them. Tune in to the frequency of an animal, open your senses, and recognize when they are communicating with you, and you have a pathway to magic. I can't help but think that Jemima stayed to eat her tetracycline-dusted food and drink her Tylan-medicated water for three weeks after she fell ill because she somehow understood that she had to, that that vital information had made it from my mind to hers. Maybe not, but maybe so. As soon as her medication course was finished, I relaxed about it all, and she did too; her visits became much more intermittent. I still marvel that I managed to get medication into a free-living bird every day for three weeks. Jemima could just as easily have vanished with the

Jemima allows my shadow to fall across her as she drinks, a sign of lasting trust. October 15.

local jays immediately upon release. Having experienced this with Caledonia and Josie in the summer of 2018, I'm all the more amazed that Jemima hung around as long as she did.

But she stayed, and that was the greatest gift of all. Remembering the uncanny ways that birds have come to me when I'm in need and turmoil, and the ways I seemingly stumble upon them when *they're* in need, I'm humbled to think that some kind of metacommunication is going on between us. I come upon hurt, lost, and broken creatures far too frequently for chance to be guiding the encounters. It could, of course, have much to do with the way I watch wild things — closely, for prolonged periods, and with a mind to their mental and physical state. But how to explain the goldfinch hopping out of the weeds to my feet, the thrasher stumbling by the side of the road, the fallen fledgling Hoffman's woodpecker outside my Costa Rican hotel window, who I fed until I reunited him with his parents the next morning? They, and so many others, regularly present themselves to me. Believing that these metaphysical lines of communication exist, knowing that animals and birds think

No peanut was too big to bear away and hide. August 7.

in pictures, and teaching myself to do so, as well, has given me a way to communicate my good intentions to birds and animals in my continual efforts to help them, and brought me experiences that have changed me.

I'd like to believe that, wherever Jemima has gone since I last saw her on Christmas Eve 2017, she is making her way. I suppose it's a blessing not to know what happened to her or where she is, how far she's hopped, fluttered, laddered, and whirred her way, for to know would be to worry her all the way home. I think of her in the company of her group. I envision them waiting for her to catch up, even choosing routes she can better navigate. As a social being, she depends on them for her very survival. If a blue jay nonchalantly hops into the secret studio feeder, which I keep stocked with goodies to this day, and fixes me with a knowing look, I'd be more than delighted to start the great engine of observation humming again and allow myself to be pulled in by the workings of its gears. I'd be the happiest person on earth, but I'm not going to hang my happiness on whether or not she returns. I'll let my connection with Jemima continue to spread into the broader communion I feel with every blue jay I see. My study of and obsession with one bird has fed into a keener awareness of everything blue jays do, everything they are. Writing this, I'm constantly grabbing the camera to make mug shots of the mob of jays at the feeding station just outside. The gray-crowned bird is unusually aggressive. Gray. The one with a little bit of silver on its forecrown has figured out the peanut feeder. Little Bit. There's one with a blank stare: no black around its eyes. Basic. Here's the one I found last winter, with a break in its black necklace. Gap. And I'm always watching for my beloved Frost. If Jemima taught me anything, it's to love what I have. The ones we love most may leave, but feeling bereft about it is a choice.

As I was wrapping up Jemima's story, it was fall migration

time, and everywhere I went, I saw flocks of blue jays, threes and twenties and hundreds, streaming over. I couldn't guess where they were bound, but they were going, some carrying an acorn snack for the trip. At hawk-watch sites, people count them in the thousands. Having had the privilege of being mama to four, I knew as I looked up that in each cranium, under each one of those thousands of pointed crests, was one of the most remarkable brains in the animal kingdom. That is a lesson and a gift all its own.

Although it's hard to choose a favorite photo, this one comes closest to capturing Jemima's brilliant, brave spirit. November 10.

In the meantime, I'm keeping tabs on Frost, who reappeared in October 2018 and wound up nesting here, and I keep peanuts and mealworms in Jemima's feeder at all times, much to the delight of the titmice, cardinals, and Carolina wrens. The birds I once considered dread pirates have become the whole point now. I love calling them in for a wriggly treat. I won't leave my post. I can't. I'm in the catbird seat here, just looking out at the birds in my yard, witnessing their small dramas unfolding every day. I'm obsessively building my dossier of dated jay mug shots, and the gallery of individuals I can recognize grows every week. I don't know where it's all headed, but it's somewhere I'm glad to go. Still, I'll savor every memory of the blue jay who came just when I needed her most, pulled me back out of despair and into my real work, was sick and made well again, stayed to wish me a Merry Christmas, and left me here to stitch together her story, saving Jemima in words and pictures for us all.

Little Bit
- Deep blue, white face
- Little bit of forecrown spangling
- Spiky lower throat margin
- White band at primary coverts

Sparkle
- Round spangling on forecrown
- White face
- Deep blue
- Smooth throat margin
- No white at primary coverts.

Gray
· Pallid, greyish overall
- Pale grey crown
- Messy, spiky brow band
- Aggressive

Frost
- Copious forecrown white
- Contrasting whitish breastband on dark underparts

Jemima
- Slight blobby "y" on right eyebrow mark
- Otherwise, generic.

Gap
- Extra long throat feathers interrupt black necklace
- Gray face, throat.

Maybelline
- Round crown
- Slight forecrown white
- Heavy face markings
- Dark underparts

Peg
- No black browband
- Extra-long facial feathers and fluffy nasal tufts
- Thin necklace (obscured by long throat feathers)

TWENTY

Step into My Parlor

IT IS MY hope that, having read this book, you're seeing jays in a deeper, more appreciative and more inquisitive way than you might have before. I will give no ink to tired old prejudices against blue jays; as greedy, loud, overbearing omnivores, humans dwell in a glass house. I wish there were a *Big Book of Blue Jays* I could recommend for further reading, but it has yet to be written. With this final chapter, I hope to push the door open a little wider for anyone who, curiosity piqued, wants to step farther into their world.

A small sampling of the individual jays I can recognize as of late 2018. Subtle differences in a constellation of facial features contribute to each bird's distinctive look.

APPEARANCE

What is a blue jay? *Cyanocitta cristata* is a small, brightly colored, fascinating corvid, eleven inches long, with a sixteen-inch wingspan, weighing around three ounces. I'd love to know what percentage of that is brain. Colored with splashy precision in "them baseball clothes o' his" — as poet James Whitcomb Riley put it — the blue jay is a symphony in black, white, gray, and myriad shades of blue, from cerulean to cobalt. White tips all but the central two tail feathers, showing as a snowy V in flight, and forms two bands on the spread wing. A black necklace runs from the crest, down the sides of the neck, and across the breast. Black eyebrow, forecrown, and eye lines give each bird a subtly distinct look.

AGING JAYS

Juvenile jays in their first summer of life are distinguishable by fluffier, messier, and less distinctly marked plumage, including dull grayish facial markings and a moth-eaten look that progresses until their first post-juvenal molt begins in August.

Show a blue jay to a birder from Britain or Europe, and prepare to catch them as they faint. Note the barred primary coverts, revealing this bird as an after-hatch-year adult.

Then sparkling periwinkle-blue feathers replace the gray-blue of body and crest, and fresh, boldly marked tertial feathers mark the hindwings. Juvenal flight feathers are retained until August of their second year. Even after this first post-juvenal molt, they can be aged by looking at their primary coverts. Juveniles have no black barring on this tiny fan of feathers at the base of the primaries, while older (after-hatch-year) birds show fine black barring. Binoculars and a telephoto lens are necessary for finding this distinction. But other things change as blue jays age. After-hatch-year birds have much larger white tips on their tail feathers than do juvenile birds. And I'm working on a theory, borne out by my photos of known-age birds, that the white tips on tertials and greater secondary coverts get larger with each successive molt. At the same time, the pale gray brow fan, nasal tuft feathers, and even the throat feathers apparently lengthen with age. This, in turn, covers up more of the heavy black face and neck markings that often make hatch-year jays look like they are wearing too much makeup. I am developing a way of quickly aging jays not just by scrutinizing the fine barring on their primary coverts, but also by looking at the bird as a whole. I am trying to look at jays as I suspect they look at each other. My belief is that the array of highly variable facial markings blue jays exhibit, which seem to stay consistent, with subtle changes as the birds age, serves to identify individuals while imparting information about their age—something vital to a highly social species.

SEXING JAYS/VOICE

There's no visual way for humans to tell the sexes apart; though males average 3 percent larger, there is much overlap. Only witnessing courtship feeding (males feed females, not the other way around) or copulation (male on top!) makes it possible to discern who's who. Both sexes give a wide range of jeering screams, hawk imitations, and burbling bell calls. Since courtship and copulation are usually conducted away from prying eyes, what's a curious corvid addict to do? There are two sex-specific calls to the rescue, but you have to be alert to notice them. Male blue jays give a high, whining, two-part "squeaky-gate" call, most frequently in early spring. This is not to be confused with the common, burbling *teedle-oo* or *skirdlp!* call. The male jay's squeaky-gate call is a distinctive two-part whine that drops at least an octave on the second note. The sex-specific call of female blue jays is a low, toneless, doubled purring growl, the bird bobbing comically as she produces it.

RANGE

Blue jays range across the eastern two-thirds of the continental United States and Canada, reaching their range limit along the eastern borders of Montana, Wyoming, and New Mexico. They are breeding sporadically farther west, though, pushing toward the Pacific Northwest with increasing frequency. For blue jay lovers, that can only be good news. It's thought that the westward range expansion is linked to widespread bird feeding. As opportunistic omnivores, blue jays eagerly exploit a wide variety of artificial foods and set up ephemeral winter camps wherever they find feeding stations. As feeders go, so, it seems, go jays.

MIGRATION

Blue jays are assumed to be largely year-round residents wherever they occur, though many move around starting in fall, birds from the north possibly switching places with resident birds, who may then push farther south or west. The migration picture for blue jays is anything but clear, even though massive flocks can be seen moving determinedly south and west in September. The mystery of where they go and who goes — why jay migration seems to be optional, just for some birds in some years — will intrigue humans as long as we watch and wonder. While there are blue jays present year-round here in southeast Ohio, my observations indicate that, starting in November, the cast of characters occupying my yard changes every two to three weeks. It's as if there is a pot full of blue jays that gets stirred occasionally. This is a supposition that's unsubstantiated by hard data — such as banding or color marking — but it's an informed supposition. More on my methods below.

DIET

A widely varied diet, revealed in an epic 1922 examination of 530 blue jay stomachs (Beal 1922), was comprised of 22 percent insects, year-round. Nuts, mostly acorns but also beech, hickory, chestnuts, and hazelnuts, comprised 43 percent of the diet, while fruits made up 7 percent. Cultivated grains rounded out the balance. A modern analysis of 530 blue jay stomachs (heaven forfend!) would doubtless find sunflower, peanuts, and cracked corn in abundance as this opportunistic bird embraces the banquet we offer. In the 1922 study, traces of eggs and nestlings were found in only 6 of 530 samples, despite the fact that a major focus of the study was determining the extent of jay carnivory. That's about 1 percent of 530 jays. You can use that statistic on the next jay hater who attempts to blacken their name.

TERRITORY

Blue jays are not territorial in the traditional sense; they neither sing at nor defend boundaries. The authors of the online

Birds of North America's species account put it this way: "'Territoriality' in blue jays may be better conceived as dominance contests that are repeated between neighbors, rather than as defense of discrete space." In other words, jays are more concerned with their social standing in the neighborhood than with keeping the yard all to themselves. They appear to be long-term monogamists. Divorce has been observed in only two of twenty-eight known mated pairs.

BREEDING

Watch for female solicitation (crouching with wings dropped and spread, bill inclined upward, and quiet, keening *kew kew kew* calls) of a female jay asking for attention from her mate; it may precede copulation. Jays are famously secretive and silent when nesting; they are so wary and watchful that they may build a nest in your yard without your ever knowing. They select a wide variety of tree species, branch types, and heights for nesting; nest sites are as unpredictable as jays themselves. Someone sent me photos of jays nesting on a small shelf on her Ohio back porch,

May 11: Watch for jays with wet, soiled breasts in spring; these will be females, who have been shaping their nest cups with their bodies.

a move one might better expect from a robin. The nest is strong and substantial, with a base of fine twigs, often torn live from branches, grading into compressed wet leaves, mud, and ending with a cup of fine dark rootlets pulled from freshly exposed earth. Average clutch size is four greenish, heavily speckled eggs, which are incubated for around seventeen days. The female alone incubates; the male takes care of all her food needs, so a bird repeatedly seen departing a feeder with gullet-loads of food in spring and early summer may be assumed to be a male.

YOUNG BIRDS

Blue jays hatch naked and pink, their skin soon turning dark gray. The gape is red. Pinfeathers begin to emerge on the wing stubs by Day 3. The eyes begin to open by Day 7, and the bird resembles a spiny porcupine until Day 11, when feathers along the back and sides are breaking out of their sheaths. By Day 14, the sides of the head and throat are beginning to feather out. Fledging usually occurs from Day 17 to 21. Fledglings are not capable of sustained flight but can flutter-hop, and it is at this stage that many run afoul of unrestrained cats and dogs or are abducted from their families by well-meaning people. Confining all pets and lifting grounded fledglings into low tree branches is the best thing to do; their parents will find them. Fledglings travel; most are more than seventy-five feet away from the nest tree by their second day out of the nest, when they can usually avoid capture by people. Within a week of leaving the nest, sustained flights of sixty feet or more and increasingly adept landings keep them mostly out of harm's way. Young are fed for one to two months after fledging. It's not known when wild jays achieve full independence from their parents, but Jemima was picking up her own food and ready for release around Day 38. Constant food subsidy meant that she wasn't truly independent, but by Day 38, she had all the skills she needed to be on her own. With their long juvenile dependency period, blue jays usually have time for but one brood per season.

ATTRACTING JAYS

As Jemima taught me, omnivores are fun to feed! Feeding blue jays takes a little adjustment. Because they gather, bear away, and cache most of the food they pick up, jays can come off as terrible gluttons. If you have a flock at your feeders, it behooves you to put out large amounts of lower-cost foods, saving the expensive nuts and homemade dough for treats. Blue jays will

A special feeder for peanut halves makes jays work for their treat, and keeps them from gobbling them all. I've retrofitted mine with a plastic saucer to catch fragments for the Carolina wrens.

try almost anything, but here are a few sure-fire jay attractants.

Peanuts in the shell are quickly borne away and stashed, rarely hammered open on the spot. *Shelled peanuts* are a gourmet treat, to be parsed out sparingly. A good bird-feeding store should have both in bulk, though they are usually sold raw. I serve all peanuts roasted, to eliminate any harmful molds, which is why my house smells of roasting peanuts all winter long. *Black oil sunflower* and *sunflower hearts* are taken by jays, but when given a choice, they gravitate toward peanuts and corn. *Whole corn* sends jays into a frenzy of gobbling, filling their gullets for caching. *Cracked corn* is always popular and, like whole corn, is very affordable when bought in bulk (around eight dollars for a fifty-pound bag at feed stores).

One blue jay treat I offer is a bit odd: crumbled *baked eggshells*. Jays have a thirst for calcium, and they eagerly accept eggshells. I keep a tin pan in my oven so I can sterilize them for consumption. Every time I crack an egg, I rinse the shells and toss them in the pan. The next time I fire up the oven, those

A jay makes like a woodpecker at the suet cage, to the disgust of the resident hairy woodpecker.

collected shells get baked and sterilized. I remove them before they turn brown, put them in a jar, and shake it vigorously to break the shells into edible bits. I toss handfuls up onto my garage roof, and sprinkle them on landscape stones for the birds to find. Females of many species eat them: warblers, gnatcatchers, tanagers, and finches in breeding season — but barn swallows and blue jays are my most enthusiastic customers. Blue jays, alone among birds, eagerly eat them year-round. Blue jays have been observed eating chips of white latex paint off houses, and the jay I call Sparkle has a penchant for eating perlite from the potting mix I dump in my flower beds. I try to keep Sparkle and friends in calcium-rich eggshells.

Though jays will eagerly bear off baked goods, I strongly discourage feeding bread or sweets like doughnuts or jelly — empty calories — to wild birds. It's far better to clean the cupboard and offer those *mixed nuts* that are a bit past their freshness date. Some jays develop a taste for *suet* and *suet blocks*. Some people offer *dry kibble* (cat or dog) with success.

Zick Dough, adapted from my friend Carrie Griffis's recipe, is a nutritious high-energy treat to offer jays and many others in the depths of winter.

ZICK DOUGH

Combine (in mixer if desired):

2 cups unmedicated chick starter (available at farm and feed stores)

2 cups quick oats

1 cup yellow cornmeal

1 cup flour

Melt together in microwave:

2 cups lard (available in tubs at Walmart)

1 cup peanut butter

Slowly add liquid fats to dry ingredients while stirring or mixing until dough forms. If it's too gummy, add more flour and cornmeal until it's soft and crumbly. Serve as a treat in a dish or dome feeder to protect from rain. Store in jars. Needs no refrigeration. Offer only in cold weather, as it's too rich for summer feeding.

A FEEDER FOR JAYS

Being large and boisterous, blue jays aren't fond of swinging dome or tube feeders. They need something solid to land and bounce around on. In Jemima's winter, I hit upon using a couple of cinder blocks set on end as an impromptu jay feeder, and they proved so popular that in the winter of 2018 I expanded it

CyanoCity is an ephemeral installation of cinder blocks, catering to boisterous blue jays (and lining them up nicely for observation).

into a six-block complex. My nerdy name for it is CyanoCity. At any given time, I can see up to nine *Cyanocitta cristata* happily plumbing the blocks for the usual fare and their daily surprises. I'm aware that cinder blocks aren't considered attractive garden ornaments. CyanoCity's beauty dwells entirely in its functionality. In wet weather, the square compartments in each upright block keep the food mostly dry and unsullied by droppings. The feeder really comes into its own in snow, and when festooned by whirling blue jays, it is a thing of Bauhausian beauty, an installation of found, recycled materials with an ever-changing cast of live actors. At least that's how I think of my corvine Stonehenge, which will be installed each winter from here on out.

ENJOYING BLUE JAYS MORE

I can't get enough of blue jays, and my fascination with them only deepens. I started photographing them with intent in Jemima's summer, and that passion has snowballed into thousands of digital images made each month. I date the photos, label them, and store them away like a jay caches acorns. But there's a method in my apparent madness. As told in "Peg and Me," I've come to realize that it is possible to distinguish some blue jays from all the others. And I've found that each time I go back into my photographic archives, I'm startled to recognize a few birds that had heretofore blended into the pack.

I use a Canon EOS 80D with a 70–300mm zoom lens. I do virtually all my wild jay photography through my studio windows. Though there are a lucky few, like Lesley the Bird Nerd, who can hand-feed their (year-round resident) jays, I'm not so lucky. My cast of actors changes so frequently that taming them is an impossible dream. And stalking them outside is an exercise in futility; it's best to attract them with food and shoot from inside the house. Overcast lighting is best for blue jay observation and photography, as the subtle shading of their plumage and differences in color show to best effect in diffuse light. Overcast snowy days are best of all.

If you look at enough jays, and keep a dossier of photos of them, subtle distinguishing characteristics in their plumage begin to settle out. I'll break these down one by one.

1. **Overall color:** Some jays are grayer; some are paler; some are just darker and bluer than others. A few individuals in a flock will jump out at you for differences in their overall coloration. Note them well, and move on to other plumage characteristics.

2. **Face color:** Some jays have grayish faces and throats; some are bright whitish. The white-faced ones will really stand out with time and observation.

3. **Brow fan:** The semicircle of pale gray feathers above the eye. This can be wide and fluffy or small and low; when it's long and spiky in front, it gives the bird a surprised look.

4. **Nasal tufts:** Rounded feather tufts covering the nostrils. Note their color and size. They range from whitish to dark gray to bluish. Some, like Peg, have larger, fluffier nasal tufts than others, to the extent that the brow band can be completely obscured by the tufts.

5. **Forecrown:** The forecrown is right above the bristly nasal tufts. It can be whitish, grayish, or blue, but a certain percentage of jays have white spangling on the forecrown. This is called "progressive graying," and it is analogous to a dog's muzzle and eyebrows, which turn silvery as it ages. Progressive graying can show up on a juvenile bird, too. Note the distribution of the white spangles. These may become more extensive as the bird ages. Of all identification characteristics, I find forecrown color to be the quickest identifier. If a bird shows white spangling here, you're on a fast road to singling it out from the others.

6. **Brow band:** The narrow black band just above the nasal tufts. It may or may not have a projection in the middle, which I refer to as the "widow's peak."

7. **Brow spike:** Black pointed projection, running up the side of the forecrown in front of the eye. It can be short and triangular, blunt and squarish, long and tapered, or even bloblike.

8. **Loral stripe:** Black. Connected to the brow spike, the loral stripe runs between eye and nasal tuft. It can be thin or wide, even absent.

9. **Postocular stripe:** Black. Runs behind the eye toward the back of the crest. Most are quite thin; some birds have heavier postocular stripes.

10. **Eye:** Pay attention to the size, shape, and slant of the eyes. There is a surprising amount of variation, which changes the bird's individual look.

11. **Necklace:** Black, runs from back of crest, down side of head, and across chest. This is a highly changeable marking and can't reliably be used for ID. It can appear very broad when the jay's neck is stretched, or completely disappear when the bird pulls its neck in and puffs its feathers out. That's because the whitish face and throat feathers lie on top of the black necklace, and thus are able to obscure it. In rare cases, exceptionally long throat feathers can break the necklace's outline even when the neck is stretched, as in the bird I call Gap.

12. **Bib margin:** The interface between whitish throat feathers and black necklace. It can be smooth or notably spiky. A few birds show a blue sheen on the lower throat.

The white flash on his primary flight feathers is an instant shortcut to Little Bit's identification, but I check the other markers to be sure.

13. **Apron:** The pale zone on the upper breast just beneath the necklace. Note the shape of the apron and the degree of contrast between the pale apron and the gray flanks.

14. **Flanks:** The gray side panels on the breast. Some are darker than others.

The best way to start trying to distinguish individual jays is to pick a bird who exhibits distinctive behavior. Perhaps you have one with a penchant for the peanut feeder who's bolder than the rest. Scrutinize and photograph this bird. I call my peanut-lover Little Bit. Having seen this bird give the squeaky-gate male call, I know his sex. Luckily, he's a distinctive jay, an after-hatch-year adult who has overall deep blue coloration, a white face, a high spiky brow fan, small whitish nasal tufts, a "little bit" of silver on his forecrown, a wide brow band with a slight widow's peak, heavy brow spikes, wide loral and post-ocular stripes, a spiky bib margin, a thin pale apron, and dark flanks. A rare white flash just below the primary coverts of the wing rounds out a unique bird.

If that sounds like a lot of things to keep track of, well, it is! I don't mean to overwhelm you; just to show you all the factors that can go into identifying an individual jay. It's all far too much for anyone to memorize. That's where the camera comes in! Let your photographs remember all that, while the information slowly osmoses into your brain.

Birds who have one highly distinctive marker, like Frost's all-silver forecrown, Gap's broken necklace, or Little Bit's white primary slash, are comparatively easy to nail down. And

I followed this jay for part of an autumn afternoon, intrigued by its distinctive face. Long crest feathers flop down and obscure its brow fan, giving it an apparently permanent blue Beatle wig and a rakish air.

then there are the rest who, at first blush, give you nothing to hang your hat on. It's only by the combination of more than a dozen subtle characteristics that I can arrive at an identification of rather generic individuals. For now, I'm concentrating on the birds with a few distinctive features that I can remember easily. But as I gain confidence, I'm casting a wider net. After I've identified an individual enough times, comparing its profile photos, I form a mental picture of that bird. I begin to recognize it when I see it.

Then I refer to my archived photos in a file called Blue Jay-Mugshots. And having done this many times with many birds, powerful magic is happening. It's an exhilarating feeling to have a jay plop down in front of you and suddenly recognize its face, just as you'd spot a human friend in a crowd. To me, identifying blue jays is a fun, thrilling, and compelling game, with the enormous bonus of learning something about that individual bird and blue jays in general. It's the same urge, I think, that leads so many people to online gaming. I've come to suspect that the phenomenal success of eBird has to do with tying the addictive qualities of gaming — the human urge to chart our small successes — in to a quest for useful ornithological data. Why not channel the same addictive quest into observing blue jays?

Be sure to date your best jay shots and label them with the name you've given the bird. I recommend simple names that recall the most distinctive feature of the bird (Wash, Gap, Gray, Sparkle, Frost . . .). To help anchor your IDs, it's really useful to make a sketch for quick reference. I've created a blank template of a jay, with faint indications of where the markings fall. I'd recommend making multiple copies of this sheet (found at the very back of the book) so you can make jay mug shots to your heart's content. Make notes about plumage characteristics and behavior next to each mug shot. When you've got some jays nailed down, post the sheet near the window overlooking the feeders. You might want to fill in the markings in pencil; like mine, your results will vary, and your accuracy will improve the more you watch.

It's no accident that the most thorough studies of blue jays originate in places where the birds are apparently year-round residents: Keith Tarvin and Glen Woolfenden's work at

Archbold Biological Station in south Florida; and Lesley the Bird Nerd's photo and video documentation of blue jays in Newfoundland. If blue jays hate anything, they hate crossing large bodies of water, so the birds in these places seem to stay put—a great boon to research. Southeast Ohio, where I live, seems to be a blue jay corridor, and my gang of jays changes over every few weeks all winter long, my visitors flying happily overland. It's disorienting to get a good number of jays individually identified, only to have a brand-new flock swoop in and replace them. The newcomers not only look different; they behave differently, frantically gobbling grain and seed as if they're afraid the riches they've just discovered will vanish. I flounder for a few days and then settle into the challenge of trying to sort them out. If my experience with Peg, Little Bit, and Frost is indicative, the same birds might be expected to return winter after winter. The more I can put a name to, the more fun I'll have. As I wrap up the last chapter, it's a freezing cold December 11, and I've nailed down eight jays I know: Little Bit, Puff, Gray, Marine, Gap, Wash, Sparkle, and good old Frost. Epic! My old friends have come in to cheer me across the finish line. Yes, Jemima moved on, but she's left me an entire clan for company.

I hope these pointers will help guide you should you decide to take the plunge into identifying individual jays. It's a gentle, deeply absorbing pursuit, and you can't help but learn a great deal about blue jays as you study them closely. My studies are punctuated by frequent yelps of laughter as my subjects boing around, jump on each other's heads, and try to get as much food in their gobs as possible. Jays are joy, jays are laughter; jays are brilliant, bold, and flamboyant. You could do worse than to spend your days staring at blue jays.

SOURCES

Beal, Foster E. L. *Farmers' Bulletin No. 630: Some Common Birds Useful to the Farmer* (US Department of Agriculture, 1922).

Riley, James W. "Knee-deep in June." In *Knee-deep in June and Other Poems* (Indianapolis, IN: Bobbs Merrill, 1912).

Much information in this account from Tarvin, Keith A., and Glen E. Woolfenden. "Blue Jay (*Cyanocitta cristata*)." In *The Birds of North America*, no. 469, A. Poole and F. Gill, eds. (Philadelphia, PA: Birds of North America, Inc., 1999).

EPILOGUE

I WAS WORKING on the last painting for this book on December 16, 2018, when the severe stomach pain my husband, Bill Thompson III, had endured since September was finally diagnosed as pancreatic cancer, stage IV. Down we all descended, into a whirlpool of grief and loss. There was a month or so after his diagnosis during which we were bathed in a witch's brew of terror, despair, and disbelief. I described what was going on for my friends as living in a continually flushing toilet, hanging onto the slick rim, trying not to go down with the flood of bad news being thrown at us. Escape was not an option. Everything that attends the possible end of life: pain, fear, despair, the loss of individual freedom and choice; the worry about what will become of one's legacy — all those things became our constant companions. The only way through this was straight ahead.

We underwent a painful recalibration of our concept of normal, which is akin to lifting the covers on your warm bed and allowing a large Komodo dragon — cool, scaly, deadly — to slither its way under and lie down at your side. We were still here in the familiar surrounds of our homes, trying to lead our lives, but cancer had curled around us, demanding homage and vigilant attention. We were forced to lie down with the dragon, to surrender to whatever was coming, no matter how tragic, unfair, or terrible. I had spent most of the last fourteen years buffering and shielding our children as our marriage ever so slowly came apart, but I was caught without tools for this job. And it turned out that everyone stepped up and faced it in their own way, and that honesty, compassion, and love — always more love — were the only tools I had, and the only ones I needed. To dive in and support Bill's partner, Wendy, as she cared for him twenty-four hours a day was my privilege. Her life experience and formidable intellect armed her for the worst, and her lionhearted devotion humbled everyone who witnessed it. I am deeply grateful our bonds had stretched but never broken; that we lived but a pleasant hike apart; that in health and now in sickness I could offer love, diversion, food, logistical support, and help with chores. The steady stream of visitors from far away stayed with me, their great love and admiration for Bill a concrete testament to his vast influence in the world of birding.

We brought Phoebe and Liam home as much as we could but asked that they return to their beautiful lives — Liam studying art at West Virginia University, and Phoebe living and teaching in the Canary Islands — to best help us get through it. Out of it, there eventually emerged a kind of altered normalcy, because, we've found, you can't stay in continual crisis. You pick up what pieces of your life you can still recognize and forge on. Though everything conspired to pull me away, I was determined not to lose track of the blue jays, for watching them even for a few minutes brought me home to the old me, the curious, questing, wildly passionate student at their shiny black feet. I bought peanuts and corn and sunflower seed; I kept Cyano-City stocked. I photographed jays whenever I could grab the time. As always, I watched for the ones I could recognize, and thrilled to the ones I couldn't. I kept making mug shots. I learned incrementally more about blue jays with each encounter.

February 9, 2019, dawned bright and sunny, and an old friend had come to visit. Jim McCormac, a storied naturalist who'd recently retired from the Ohio Division of Natural Resources, had come to spend time with Bill. The two were downstairs recording a conversation for one of Bill's popular podcasts, *This Birding Life*. Bill interviewed Jim, then Jim turned the tables, asking one of the world's most effective birding evangelists about his work.

It was quiet in my studio, and I was perched lightly in the catbird seat, watching and photographing jays. Within minutes, I realized that though it was sprinkled with a few familiars like my beloved Frost, this was a new flock. I was seeing birds I hadn't seen for months, and some who were brand-new. Or were they? There was Black Velvet Band, an unmistakable bird I had photographed only once before. There was Gray, a big, aggressive, pale bird I hadn't seen for many weeks. Around 10:30 a.m., a jay startled me by landing in the evergreen just outside the window, less than a yard away from me as I sat at my drawing table. My heart leapt and banged against my breastbone. In all my years of watching, no jays other than Jemima and Maybelline had ever landed on that branch, which I thought of as Jemima's alone. I wheeled. The camera clicked. Through the lens, I had seen something that stilled my leaping heart. It was the forked right brow mark that only one jay had consistently shown. That jay had been Jemima.

I quelled a scream. The bird dropped down to gobble corn and peanuts I'd left on the landscaping stones. It flew repeatedly out toward the orchard to cache, then return. It landed on the peanut feeder and wrestled a peanut out — not something a naïve jay tries on its first visit to the yard. This bird clearly knew its way around. It returned to the heated birdbath casually, comfortably, drinking at length. It gathered more whole corn and, before my unbelieving eyes, cached little troves of it in the lawn right by the birdbath. I'd never seen any jay but Jemima do that; wild ones had always carried their booty out of the yard and hidden it in the woods. It perched again in the evergreen just a few feet from me as I stood, agog and clearly visible, making dozens of images. Its companion followed suit, perching close by. And that bird looked strangely familiar, as well. I could only grab images and plan to compare their likenesses later. I knew the analysis would be the work of days, a labor of love, curiosity, and passion. My true work.

When Bill and Jim finally came upstairs and walked into the studio, I was incoherent and babbling with excitement. I pushed binoculars into their hands. "There's a pair of jays here and I-I-I-I th-th-th-think it's J-J-Jem and Maybelline I-I-I th-th-think she's back I think it's them! L-L-L-Look at that one see the forked brow prong, that's Jem I think and it's acting like Jem it's so familiar and unafraid!! It was perched right HERE right next to the window!!"

Bill's face lit up in unalloyed joy; I hadn't seen him smile like that, like the very sun, for so long. We hugged and wept and high-fived. "She's back! She came back!" But oh! It was too good to be true. I didn't want to pounce on false hope. It would take me days of close comparison of my photos of Jemima, when I'd last seen her, and this bird I referred to as Prime Suspect, to feel justified in believing Jemima might have made it through her ordeal and come home. My heart screamed YES! My head said SLOW DOWN!

I was thrilled to go back through my rogue's gallery of

April 1, 2019: Prime Suspect Jemima shows a distinctive forked right brow mark and perfect flight feathers.

blue jay mug shots, to find Black Velvet Band and Gray photographed on the same days in November 2018. So these birds were traveling together. In that same flock on November 13, I had photographed two jays that, for lack of any more information, I'd labeled Basic and Beauty. They seemed to be a pair. I gasped as I recognized in those November images the two birds I now suspected, by both markings and behavior, to be Jemima (Basic) and Maybelline (Beauty). The world spun around me. I enlarged their photos to see that both displayed the barred primary coverts of birds more than one year old. They were in the correct age class to be Jem and Maybelline! Had they returned? Had I found the flock that spirited them away? Were these the birds who had waited up for my tattered darling as she laddered and churned her way south, or west, or east? Could Jemima have survived seven more months — half a winter and the whole next summer — flying on a quarter of the wing feathers she needed?

Well, in her defense, she had already survived five months of that — I'd documented it daily, from early August to the end

Prime Suspect Jemima shows distinctive field marks: a forked right brow mark, and white upper tail coverts. March 21, 2019.

of December. Her primary feathers had been largely broken off when I first discovered her disability on August 9, 2017. She'd compensated so well I hadn't even noticed a difference in her flight until I saw the broken feathers. But when she disappeared at Christmas, she was flying so poorly and with such effort that I figured it was unlikely I'd ever see her again. The bad cards were simply stacked too high.

My blue jay study is an all-absorbing pastime. I'm in it for the long run. By photographing every jay I can and carefully curating thousands of their images, I am building, block by tiny block, a citadel of information. I save photos, knowing each is a loose piece in a vast puzzle. I may not know where each piece fits for months or years. By saving, naming, and dating my images, I'm creating retrievable data points. This is how science is carried out, data point by data point. *Eureka!* moments are an intermittent reward, but they come often enough to keep me, the hopeful lab rat, pushing that pedal, knowing that sooner or later a pellet will fall into my hands. Insights and epiphanies pop up when I least expect them. I'm figuring out, bit by bit, who travels with whom, and how long they travel before revisiting a certain location. I'm beginning to know how jays may tell each other apart; how changes in their plumage visibly display their age. In my painfully slow, human way, I'm picking up on subtleties that have heretofore been a well-kept corvine secret. All this arcane knowledge makes not a blip on anyone else's radar screen. That makes it all the more precious to me. I feel as though all those hours of poring over photographs of dozens of individual birds was preparing me for exactly this moment, when two strange jays flew into the yard. Being jays, they and their flock hung around for two days, then took off with the next warm front, leaving me to work the puzzle, to hope for their return.

Because they aren't banded, I may never know for certain if my two prime suspects are truly Jemima and Maybelline. But they sure do look and act like them. And the probability that a bonded pair of after hatch-year blue jays with markings that match Jem's and Maybelline's would suddenly appear, make use of the facilities, and nonchalantly perch where they always

Prime Suspect Jemima was gagging down peanuts as this book went to press. March 31, 2019.

did — where no other blue jays have perched since they left — is pretty darn low. Caching corn in the lawn? Pure, dopey Jemima stuff.

The poet in me weeps with joy. The scientist in me, while ready to be proven wrong, has done the analysis and concluded it looks good.

I could be wrong. But if I'm right . . . well, there's a burst of sweetness, light, and hope that my family and I sorely need. There, perhaps, flies a hand-raised blue jay, fully wild and pair-bonded, despite her bizarre start in life: singing along to pop music, hopping from arm to arm, pestering an elderly dog. There's a fully wild bird with perfect feathering, cured of *Mycoplasma*. If that bird is Jemima, there's a real survivor, who flew and foraged and lived for a year — perhaps even migrated! — on terribly tattered wings. As I write on April 1, 2019, Prime Suspect Jemima is stuffing her craw with peanuts and corn, like it's no big thing to sputter off on broken wings and return fourteen months later, whole and healed. If a bird can survive all that, and lift us, too, on now-flawless wings, there is truly something wonderful at work in the world.

Bill took his last breath at home on March 25, 2019, with our arms around him. His family gathered around, and we had spent the evening singing songs and telling stories for him. It had all happened so fast — three months and one week from diagnosis, he was leaving us, the cancer spreading like a grass-fire in his body. If there was anything to be salvaged from the wreckage, it was that his friends and family were able to tell him that he is loved beyond measure: not a chance many of us get. We threw him a musical birthday blowout on March 3, when he somehow summoned the energy to sing and play guitar with his friends and bandmates for eleven hours straight. He heard from multitudes who said he'd changed their lives with his al-ways-open arms, welcoming new birders with his books, pod-

Prime Suspect Jemima fixes a bright eye on the author as the epilogue is rewritten, April 1, 2019. Note forked right brow mark.

casts, and the family magazine, *Bird Watcher's Digest.* He knew, though, that even as he's brought the joy of birdwatching to thousands of people, Phoebe and Liam are his finest work and legacy. And I know to my core that he's found out what it is the brilliant Apple founder Steve Jobs saw as he drew his last breaths. Taken too soon from Earth by the same dragon we fought, Jobs could only look into the distance, breathing, "Oh wow. Oh wow. Oh wow."

> *Even after all this time,*
> *The sun never says to the earth,*
> *"You owe me."*
> *. . . Look what happens with*
> *A love like that.*
> *It lights the whole sky.*

> — HAFIZ OF PERSIA

INDEX

DATE DUE

SEP 13 2019

SEP 3 0 2019	
WITHDRAWN	